What people are saying about

# Making Sense of Brief Lives

I would love to see *Making Sense of Brief Lives* on the syllabus for all first year seminary students. Smoke does readers a service by repeatedly focusing attention on matters of utmost existential relevance and providing clear and simple tools to address them. In doing so, Smoke is uncompromising in his honesty and merciless in assailing wishful thinking on all fronts. In an age when so many in our culture cannot muster the internal resources to reflect critically on their commitments, this is a call that needs to be made again and again. A supernaturalist account of religion is regularly examined in these pages. Like many students entering seminary, he has rightly discerned that the gods of religion are, without exception, human creations. There are a few classic ways that people respond to this realization. Smoke shows us the path of the nihilist. He feels compelled to drive the shock of existential abandonment from God's death straight through the heart of all reality. There are other paths that people of radical honesty have open to them, even—capitalizing on Golgotha—quite Christian ones. I hope that someday Smoke finds one. Like a young Saint Augustine, he has much of true value to teach us.

**Alexander Blondeau**, PhD in Systematic Theology

# Making Sense of Brief Lives

# Making Sense of Brief Lives

Phil Smoke

IFF
BOOKS

Winchester, UK
Washington, USA

JOHN HUNT PUBLISHING

First published by iff Books, 2022
iff Books is an imprint of John Hunt Publishing Ltd., No. 3 East Street, Alresford,
Hampshire SO24 9EE, UK
office@jhpbooks.com
www.johnhuntpublishing.com
www.iff-books.com

For distributor details and how to order please visit the 'Ordering' section on our website.

ISBN: 978 1 78904 822 3
978 1 78904 823 0 (ebook)
Library of Congress Control Number: 2021941984

A CIP catalogue record for this book is available from the British Library.

Design: Stuart Davies

UK: Printed and bound by CPI Group (UK) Ltd, Croydon, CR0 4YY
Printed in North America by CPI GPS partners

We operate a distinctive and ethical publishing philosophy in
all areas of our business, from our global network of authors to
production and worldwide distribution.

# Contents

# Introduction

You will live briefly in this world, and then you will die. You will never understand everything, or even understand most of what humanity as a whole has understood. But you will nonetheless think in certain ways, act in certain ways, live a certain life. This is the root of philosophy, or at least of philosophy as I engage in it. Such philosophy is maximally practical, being measured always by the realities of a single human life. And it is maximally general, straining to make as much sense as possible of this vast and baffling world. But at the same time it is maximally precise, striving to say exactly what is meant, to say nothing that is false, and to say frankly what is tentative or speculative or assumed. This sort of philosophy is the project of this book.

I will not attempt to reason from first principles in the way some philosophers have. Instead I will face the torrent of claims and arguments and evidence that actually confronts us in the world, and will both dig down toward fundamental justifications but also hold lightly to whatever conclusions are reached, keeping them always provisional and open to later revision or rejection. This will entail examining the influences of our psychology and our surroundings, and testing the claims we meet from scholars, scientists, journalists, politicians, preachers, and others. In view of the breadth of the world and the brevity of life, this will require a sort of triage according to what could be called philosophical or existential relevance, prioritizing what's most relevant to living. And in all this I will seek to be minimally technical, both in the interest of being accessible to all readers and in the interest of requiring discipline of myself, since jargon and other forms of technical discourse often obscure more than they illuminate, in philosophy as elsewhere.

The end result will address as directly and plainly as possible how an individual can understand and navigate the world. Nothing that is said will be said with certainty, for I see inadequate reason to be certain of even fundamentals like the logical law of non-contradiction or the existence of a world outside my own mind. But this absence of certainty will not be used to remain timid or passive. For although certainty is unattainable in general, and especially in the complex matters most relevant to human life, the realities of life still force practical decisions on such matters, regardless of how or even whether we've formulated positions on them. You will live a certain life, which will be consonant with certain beliefs and values but not with others. In this sense you cannot escape philosophy.

# Chapter 1

# Reason

To live unreflectively is to stumble through darkness, without choosing your path or knowing where it leads. But careful thought can light the way, at least dimly. And careful thought begins, in some senses, with foundational issues of logic, language, and truth. Such issues can become endless academic debates. But since our lives are not endless, endless debates are of limited use to us. I will therefore address these issues as briefly, simply, and decisively as possible, with the aim of establishing only what is necessary. My central claims will strike some readers as trivial or obvious, but making such claims explicit and giving them explicit support will close off many future prospects for confusion and evasion, and will hopefully begin to persuade those readers who don't already agree.

First, I will use the term "reality" to point to the totality of what is real or actual, whatever that may be. To a first approximation, my mind is part of reality, as is yours. Stars and planets and animals and atoms are all parts of reality. The psychological and social phenomena of religion are parts of reality, and if any religious claims about divine beings are correct, then those beings are parts of reality too.[1] Reality is, simply, whatever is. That's what I mean by the term—to just point at whatever is the case.[2]

Truth is more complicated, but not nearly as complicated as is sometimes claimed. The core of the matter involves human thought and speech aiming out at parts of reality,[3] and sometimes matching what's aimed at in some way that merits the label of truth. Roughly speaking, true beliefs and statements match reality while false ones do not. Various disputes about truth help to refine this picture, but they do not fundamentally change it.

Those who are skeptical of the idea of truth (or "objective truth," "absolute truth," "universal truth") point out that people constantly disagree about what's true, that people constantly invoke abstract truths in ways that serve their concrete interests, and that powerful people and groups throughout history have used claims about truth to maintain and wield their power. In another vein, there are points about the deep difficulties of knowing anything about reality, and about ways we feel sure of things that we should not rightly be sure of. In short, it's claimed that there are good reasons to doubt the truth of any truth claim, and good reasons to doubt the motives of any truth claimant.

With all of this I completely agree. But none of it poses a problem for the notion of truth I'm presenting. Because it could be the case that claims to know truth are often abused and often incorrect—but sometimes absolutely correct. It could be the case that believing true things is rare and difficult—but possible.

In what way exactly can our thoughts or words match reality so as to qualify as true? It may be hard to say. But it may also be unnecessary to say. Consider a spectrum of some possible relations that could obtain between reality and the human words and thoughts that aim at it. At one end of the spectrum is full pessimism or skepticism, doubting that our words and thoughts ever have much purchase on reality. At the opposite end of the spectrum is total confidence that those of our words and thoughts that are true correspond to reality in a way that's direct, simple, and obvious. There's a great deal of space between these two ends of the spectrum.

Within that space there are countless views that put distance between our thoughts and words and their targets without severing the connection altogether. There is room to see meaningful correspondence to reality while also allowing for various sorts of attenuation, approximation, and confusion.

There is room to see our words and thoughts as small, weak, crooked things, deeply conditioned by our particularities as individuals and as a species, but still able at some times to in some meaningful way match reality.

I tentatively commend to you this middle part of the spectrum. As we'll see moving forward, there are good reasons to doubt the naive optimism that thinks we can see reality exactly as it is. But there are also good reasons to doubt the extreme pessimism that thinks we fail to see reality at all.

Foremost among these reasons are the ways we're able to reach out and affect reality. From hunting and farming to manufacturing and medicine, our abilities to manipulate parts of reality suggest that we've successfully understood parts of reality, however partial or approximate that understanding might be.[4] More precisely, when our thoughts about reality enable us to control it in ways we were unable to control it before having such thoughts, this suggests that those thoughts match reality in some meaningful way.[5]

So our words and thoughts aim at reality, and are true when they meaningfully match it. One consequence is that truth is in some senses a matter of finding rather than building, of describing rather than defining, of pointing rather than creating.[6] This will inform how we proceed.

* * *

We are told, by turns, that what matters is national strength, or international cooperation, or being wealthy, or distributing wealth equitably, or being famous, or buying what famous people buy. We are told that we must turn away from worldly things and toward God, or that God rewards his[7] followers with worldly things, or that God loves everyone, or that God hates who we hate. Of paths to God, we're told that his son Jesus is the only way, or that God has no son and his prophet Muhammad is the only way, or that all religious paths lead to God, or that there is no God to be found by any path. We are told that scientific explanations remove the need for religious ones, or that science disproves religion, or that science actually supports religion, or that science and religion talk past each other, dealing with different and independent domains.

We meet, in short, countless conflicting claims about countless matters, including the most practical matters of how to understand the world and live in it. This confronts us with the need to choose among conflicting claims.

Sometimes the necessity of choosing is obvious. For example if we are told both that doing a particular thing will make us happy and that avoiding that thing will make us happy, or both that God commands something and that God forbids it, then it's perfectly clear that we can't heed both conflicting claims at once.

It's important to distinguish, though, between what looks like a conflict at first glance and what, after careful examination, proves to be the sort of sharp and intractable conflict that we call a contradiction, where there's absolutely no way for both claims to be true. We generally speak very loosely, and state only part of any proposition that we have in mind. This means that a given statement can stand for many different propositions, and a given proposition can be intended by many different statements. So it's only after we translate our loose statements into more precise propositions that we can judge whether a contradiction is actually present.

For example there appears to be a conflict between the statements "I am hungry" and "I am not hungry." But each statement is only the briefest shorthand for some fuller proposition. And those fuller propositions may not actually contradict each other, as is the case if, for example, the two statements are spoken at two different times. Or there's the issue of who is the speaker and subject of each statement, since there's no contradiction between me saying that I'm hungry while you say that you're not. In addition hunger exists along a continuum, with different points or bands on that continuum getting labeled with the same word. Taken together, this means that we can identify a genuine contradiction here only once we've established that one statement stands for the proposition that a particular person is at a particular time hungry in a particular sense (let's call this proposition P) while the other statement stands for the proposition that it's not the case that that particular person is at that particular time hungry in that particular sense (let's call this proposition ¬P).[8] Now we have a genuine contradiction. There is no way that P and ¬P can both be true.

And just as importantly, there is no way that P and ¬P can both be false. Since one proposition precisely negates the other, the two are mutually exclusive and jointly exhaustive. For any state of the world that we can imagine, one of the two will be true and the other will be false. Every point in logical space is covered by one and only one of the two propositions. The practical importance of this point is enormous, because normally, within our loose and natural ways of thinking and speaking, it's easy to frame a choice between two alternatives that are both false, and it's easy for that frame to become a prison.[9] Formulating precise propositions and genuine contradictions can help us escape.[10]

The foregoing points represent what are known as the laws of non-contradiction and the excluded middle. They are known as laws in roughly the sense of mathematical laws or laws of physics. They are thought to be things that we've discovered about reality rather than things we've legislated. In one sense this thinking is certainly correct. But in another sense it actually may not be.

Most attempts to express skepticism of the law of non-contradiction or the law of the excluded middle are mere sloppiness or evasion.[11] Sloppiness can be addressed by returning again and again to the need to spell out propositions with precision, while willful evasion can only be met with patience. But there is another sort of skepticism here that is fundamentally correct. This skepticism stems from the fact that we are essentially prisoners in our own minds. I experience sensory perceptions of a world outside my mind, and I observe logical laws that seem to be independent of my mind—but such experience and observation occur always and only within my mind. I can never reach out and take hold of anything outside my mind to compare it with what's inside my mind. I'm always dealing only with my own mind, and measuring some contents of my mind by other contents of my mind. How can I then be certain of anything about the world beyond my mind?

Ultimately I cannot. It's possible that all my perceptions result from deception by some powerful demon, as Descartes wrote about. Or for updated variations on this theme, it's possible that I am just a brain in a vat, with outside electrical and chemical stimuli causing all my mental experiences, or that I'm in a reality like those depicted in *The Matrix* or *The Truman Show*. Once such radical doubts are introduced, there is no way to remove them.

So it's here that I make my only two assumptions. I assume, first, that my sensory perceptions are in fact some sort of perceptions of some sort of external world. This will strike most readers as overwhelmingly justified and commonsensical. But for additional support, note that in practice we're all forced to assume the existence of an external world through practices like eating, staying warm, and exercising care when crossing streets. Without assuming an external world in practice, no one engages in philosophy for very long.

Second, I assume the rudiments of logic, namely the laws of non-contradiction and the excluded middle. I do grant that these could be laws of human psychology rather than laws of the wider universe. But nonetheless these laws are so immovable within our minds and within our practices of thinking and speaking that we are essentially forced to assume them.[12] We cannot conceive of a genuine contradiction, in which a single precise proposition is both affirmed and denied. And we cannot intelligibly argue against the laws of non-contradiction or the excluded middle, because the act of arguing presupposes these laws. Without them, an attempt to think or to speak cannot express one thing and exclude its alternatives. For example, I cannot claim that the sky is blue, because this attempted claim no longer excludes the claim that it's not the case that the sky is blue, and similarly the idea of blueness no longer excludes ideas of brownness or greenness. All content slips away, and the very prospect of thought collapses.

Granted, we can indeed put a contradiction into words, for example by asserting that there is water on Mars and also it is not the case that there is water on Mars. But we cannot actually think the content of such words. And moreover, while the content of an assertion like this flouts the law of non-contradiction, the act of asserting still assumes the law. For to assert a contradiction is to assert that the contradiction really is the case, and to deny all negations of the contradiction. Otherwise the assertion melts away to nothing.

So I assume the logical laws of non-contradiction and the excluded middle. And so does anyone who chooses to think about what I have to say, or to say anything in response.

With these theoretical points clarified we can return to the practical need to choose among contradictory claims. We've already noted the impossibility of heeding two contradictory pieces of advice. In light of the laws of non-contradiction and the excluded middle we can now add that if I believe two contradictory things then I must be believing something that is false.

Confronted with a contradiction, whether cast in terms of action or in terms of true and false beliefs, we are led toward issues of justification.[13] Confronted with two halves of a genuine contradiction, one of which we must embrace and the other of which we must reject, the question is how to choose. What distinguishes one half from the other? What grounds are there to embrace one and reject the other?

Anything that lends equal support to both sides of the contradiction cannot help us choose, and must necessarily be lending support to something false. And anything that supports even one false belief cannot be relied upon when seeking to hold only true beliefs.[14] So we're left with the question of what sorts of justification seem to lend support to beliefs that are true but never to any belief that is false.

What sorts of justification meet this standard? What are the contenders?

We believe things, by turns, because they strike us as plausible or satisfying; because they fit well with other things we believe; because they're supported by arguments that we find persuasive; because they're widely believed by those around us; because we grew up believing them; because they're asserted by various authority figures; because they're endorsed by various experts; because they're taught in sacred texts; because they're bound up with things we do or ways we see ourselves.[15] There are many different sorts of justification—but nearly all of them share the same weakness. They share the weakness of lending equal support to both sides of many contradictions. One group embraces a belief because it strikes them as plain common sense, while another group embraces a contradictory belief because it strikes *them* as plain common sense. One group embraces a belief because it's taught in their scriptures, while another group embraces a contradictory belief because it's taught in *their* scriptures. One group embraces a belief because it's bound up with their identity, while another group embraces a contradictory belief because it's bound up with *their* identity. And on and on.

I know of only one sort of justification without this otherwise-universal weakness. This sort of justification involves methodical examination of the world and careful reasoning about what is found through such examination. It's about evidence and reason, roughly speaking. Granted, evidence and reason are invoked by those on both sides of countless contradictions, just as surely as any other sorts of justification are invoked. But look closer. Invocations of evidence and reason that look alike on the surface can conceal differences underneath. There can be differing standards for what counts as evidence, for how evidence is gathered and interpreted, for how inferences are made, and for how assumptions are allowed in. Two bodies of thought can state identical standards but then reveal in practice that their real standards differ. And even when two bodies of thought truly do use identical standards, they can diverge radically because of just one lone assumption or piece of evidence that slips past those standards, and then supports an untold number of inferences which are perfectly valid, but which lead to false conclusions because they had a false premise.

But still reality looms. Reality is whatever it is, and is not anything that it is not. So all genuine evidence about reality that we faithfully glean will, when correctly understood, support a single picture of reality, whatever that picture may turn out to be.[16] And if somehow we can gather reliable evidence, eschew faulty evidence, avoid making false assumptions, and restrict ourselves to only valid inferences, then our conclusions will stay within the bounds of truth.

Doing so is the project of this book.

\* \* \*

In a very real sense you have been engaging in philosophy your entire life. Since infancy you've been constructing a view of the world. You entered the world hardwired to notice faces and emotions and social relations. Soon you began easily and automatically absorbing the grammar and vocabulary of your native tongue. In countless large and small ways you grew into your particular interpersonal setting, learning how to effectively jockey for parental affection and resources, and to form other social bonds and compete for social status. This included absorbing countless cultural norms and assumptions that you would explicitly notice only long after having absorbed them, if you've noticed them at all.

As you grew older, you gained increasing agency in your own development, and that development involved increasing propositional content, explicitly or implicitly. Adopting a particular childhood strategy of smiling and crying and begging, for example, does not imply many beliefs about the world, but going on to embrace the religious statements and practices of your community most certainly does. So you organically grew into a great many explicit and implicit beliefs.[17] And in any setting but the most homogeneous, you also got bombarded by countless claims out in the world, many of which you embraced and many of which you rejected.

In time you arrived at your particular present outlook, which could be called your worldview. It is almost certain that much of this worldview is inchoate and implicit. Almost no one tries to articulate and systematize everything he or she believes. But nonetheless, you have some beliefs that you could readily state; and there are other beliefs that you would quickly affirm if asked; and, in order for those two sets of beliefs to be true, there are upstream beliefs that must also be true, which could be called assumptions or presuppositions; and there are downstream beliefs that must be true, which could be called implications or consequences. Taken together, these four sets of beliefs constitute your worldview.

Or we might add a fifth set of beliefs, namely those reflected in your actions. An example of such a belief is that you might never have given any thought to the doctrines of Islam, but if you eat pork then you are in some sense assuming Islam is false.[18]

You are in some ways inevitably committed to the truth of all your beliefs.[19] This statement will strike many readers as tautological, since it seems that to believe something is precisely to believe that it is true; that's simply what belief means. But for those readers who don't take this view further analysis is needed.

Believing something involves embracing that belief and rejecting all contrary beliefs. If you believe that murder is wrong, then you embrace that belief while rejecting any contrary beliefs that excuse or praise murder. But what if you say that you believe murder is wrong, but also that you're not at all certain that that belief is true? Most such statements simply require us to speak more precisely. It is possible to believe something in a way that is tentative or agnostic or qualified but that is still a clear case of believing the thing to be true. For example, one person says that she's certain that murder is always wrong, for all people at all times. Another person says that she believes that murder is always wrong, but also that she's not certain that that belief is true, because she's not confident in any single argument for it, and she's aware that cultural norms around violence have varied widely. In this case, the differences between these two individuals lie in how confidently or qualifiedly they affirm the claim that murder is always wrong. But both of them are, in the end, affirming the same truth claim. And this dynamic holds no matter how many qualifications are put around a truth claim, and no matter how hard a speaker resists stating the truth claim plainly.

There may be certain readers who answer that they make no such claims about the wrongness of murder or anything else, and perhaps that they're not concerned with making truth claims at all. Some might even say that they are not interested in truth and just want to live their lives.

On its surface this may seem sensible and even attractive. But these sentiments are easier said than meant. Because actually taking no interest in truth would mean giving up all prospects of rejecting any truth claims you meet in the world, and giving up all prospects of embracing any others. It would mean indifference to all considerations of how the world actually is. It would mean indifference to such matters as whether anyone who you think knows or loves you actually does, and whether you actually have money in the bank or food in the pantry, and whether you're actually on a path to some religion's hell. It would mean indifference to whether there are in fact hungry refugees, raped women, tortured prisoners, abused animals, clearcut forests, rising seas, or senseless wars. It would mean shrugging when told that the sky is brown, that 2+2=5, or that genocide is noble. The human mind and heart simply recoil. Or at least most minds and hearts that I've encountered do.

If any readers are actually willing to take this sort of position, though, I have nothing further to say to them. As will be explored later, I see no moral imperatives or other normative forces pushing us to care about truth, and therefore the path of trenchantly ignoring truth is indeed open. But it is a very narrow path, and there are few, if any, who find it.[20]

Assuming that you are not among them, you are committed to the truth of all the beliefs that make up your worldview. And yet it's almost certain that with a few minutes of questioning I could demonstrate to you that some of your worldview must be false. I could do this by identifying a contradiction, from which it follows that one half of the contradiction must be false.

Often the contradiction lies right on the surface, within the beliefs you've already formulated, or at least within those that you'd affirm if asked. You might wonder how this can be, when we're unable to even think a sharp, genuine contradiction. The answer lies in the sequential way we think and speak. We move through time thinking one thing after another, saying one thing after another, in a sequential string. And normally we don't put much effort into comparing the different parts of this string with one another. This makes it easy to think one half of a contradiction today, to think the other half tomorrow, and to never realize that there is in fact a contradiction. Avoiding such realizations is even easier when one or both halves of the contradiction lie not in the beliefs you've already formulated or the beliefs you'd affirm if asked but instead in their presuppositions or implications.

On the relatively rare occasions when we are boxed in and pushed toward noticing a contradiction, whether by circumstance or by someone trying to point out the contradiction to us, we are extremely skilled at squirming away. Our minds work instantly and automatically to defend us from the discomfort of seeing the contradiction, and from the related discomforts of admitting mistakes and revising beliefs. In an instant the mind presents a way out of the perceived trap, and we find ourselves thinking or saying, with full confidence and sincerity, that there is in fact no contradiction because we didn't consciously intend to assert a contradiction, or because of unrelated matters that we expound at length but that actually do nothing to resolve the contradiction, or because the person attempting to point out the contradiction is immoral or hypocritical or stupid.[21] We do not calmly and fairly consider whether the contradiction might be real and might need to be addressed, except under rare conditions and with great effort. Instead the mind reacts like a rodeo bull, jumping and bucking to throw a rider in any way it possibly can.

This book will attempt to expose some of your contradictions. So before you are aware and without your conscious intention, your mind will violently reject parts of this book.

* * *

In addition to considering the actual worldviews of individuals we can consider possible worldviews, by which I mean worldviews that could be embraced by an individual and could conceivably turn out to be true.[22] In light of what we've seen regarding contradiction, the first demand we can make of any possible worldview is that it must be internally consistent, with no genuine contradictions, explicit or implicit.

But it's possible to spin out countless worldviews that are internally consistent but bear little resemblance to reality. Indeed that's one way to characterize much of philosophy, as well as much of religion and mythology.

Much of philosophy has another weakness relating to worldviews, which leads philosophical discourses to grow smaller and smaller as they progress, giving increasing attention to points of decreasing importance. This weakness favors those who tear down over those who build, and favors those who idly poke holes in others' claims over those who make meaningful claims of their own. This weakness is, in short, examining small sets of beliefs in isolation from the broader possible worldviews in which they exist.

I grant that there are certain benefits to this approach. It often enables constructive engagement on a narrow issue when attempts at broader engagement would collapse into misunderstanding and hostility. This approach also benefits from the specialization characteristic of academia by enabling experts on a narrow issue to weigh in on that issue without being drawn out into broader issues on which they lack expertise.

But the benefits of this approach are accompanied by costs. For this approach lulls us into looking at narrow issues in technical and conservative ways, even while we remain, in virtue of being particular humans living particular lives, committed to constructing and living out entire worldviews. Nitpicking and logic-chopping may be essential to philosophy professors seeking tenure, but those of us who are more concerned with using philosophy to understand and navigate the world must take a different approach. We must realize that an explicit disagreement on a narrow issue represents not just that explicit disagreement but also an implicit collision of two entire worldviews, or two sets of entire worldviews, that incorporate the explicit disagreement. So in important ways someone who attacks a belief does not merely attack that belief, but actually attacks all worldviews that depend upon it, and advocates one or more contrary worldviews that do not. In one sense the debate is asymmetric, with one side asserting and defending a belief while the other side attacks it. But in another sense the debate has perfect symmetry, with each side asserting a whole worldview, and bearing all the burdens that entails.[23]

These points should inspire several kinds of caution. First, we should be wary of drifting from an important and relevant question toward mere minutia and technicalities. Such drifting often involves giving too much credence to attacks by seeing only their strengths as narrow attacks while overlooking their weaknesses as broader worldviews. And it often involves abandoning efforts to formulate an answer to a question even while remaining bound in practice to live an answer. Second, those who value skepticism or simplicity should be slow to judge which side of a debate is the simpler or more skeptical side, and should attempt to make this judgment in view of whole worldviews and not only narrow debates. Finally, in considering the arguments of this book, readers should take care to move past mere nitpicking and hole-poking, which can never be fully precluded, and to squarely face the entire worldview I present, weighing it not against an unattainable ideal of certainty, but against the other entire and uncertain worldviews that are its only alternatives.

---

1.  Or those beings are, or that single being is, actually the entirety of reality, beneath appearances to the contrary; or that single being is

in some particular way the ground of all of reality other than itself; etc.

2.  This applies even with reference to claims about reality that focus on transcending or mystery or incomprehensibility. However exotic the claim, if it is in fact correct, then *that's* what I mean by the term "reality."

3.  Note that human thought and speech are also themselves parts of reality, and that the phrasing above represents the typical case in which a given thought or statement aims out at some part of reality other than itself, but the thought or statement can instead aim at itself.

4.  I do not mean to suggest that any affecting of reality suggests an understanding of reality. This is not the case. Organisms can, and generally do, affect reality purely through suites of evolved reactions, without any need for particular mental understandings.

5.  It's worth using the above definitions of "truth" and "reality" to parse a few common constructions that use these terms in alternative ways. For example, to "speak your truth" means to speak whatever parts of the truth you have access to. "My reality" means my experience of parts of reality. "Reality is subjective" means that beliefs about reality are subjective. To say that because of some cultural or intellectual trend "reality becomes subjective" is to say that because of that trend people disagree more about reality. For you to "change your reality" is for you to change your situation, i.e. to change the parts of reality that constitute your life. To say that "I have my truth and you have yours" is to say that you and I have different beliefs, or that you and I have experienced different parts of reality, or that there are some true things I know but you don't and other true things you know but I don't. These sorts of constructions seem to me to invite confusion, so I avoid them. But generally they are easy either to translate in this manner, or, if such a translation is rejected by the speaker, to expose as nonsense.

6.  It's easy to lose sight of this, and focus too much on theories or accounts or definitions as such, while giving too little attention to

what those theories or accounts or definitions point to. This leads to the twin errors of demanding too much detail and technicality, and then, in cases where those excessive demands are met, demanding too little outside justification.

7. In contexts that deal explicitly or implicitly with the beliefs of those who use masculine pronouns for God, I'll generally follow such usage.

8. Granted, in most contexts this would be an exhausting way to discuss hunger, because in most contexts there's no need for fine distinctions among levels of hunger, and there's no ambiguity about the timing or the parties. But ambiguities and fine distinctions are everywhere in philosophy.

9. Many of our false beliefs are not simply matters of affirming a proposition that we should negate or vice versa, but of formulating misguided propositions and dichotomies.

10. This stands in stark contrast to many other ways of thinking and speaking that can keep us in various prisons indefinitely. The key difference is whether we embrace or resist the prospect of clarifying and refining our ideas. Our initial ideas are often imprecise, unclear, impressionistic, approximate. And as thoughts and feelings on some particular issue swirl around inside us, they can give rise to a succession of statements that express the same proposition, or that express different propositions, or even that express incompatible propositions. But in each case it's possible for a speaker to insist on the statements themselves, perhaps because each statement still feels consonant with something swirling inside the speaker, and to resist clarifying what the statements mean or how they can fit together. But truth is a matter of what a statement says about the world, not how it feels to the speaker. The question is not whether all statements in a set are equally heartfelt, but how they fit with one another and with whatever parts of reality they're aiming at.

11. The same is true of most attempts to express skepticism about truth or reality.

12. I don't mean that we always obey these laws, because we don't. I

mean that when we explicitly consider these laws we are unable to intelligibly deny them. Or at least I've never encountered a denial that I've found intelligible.

13. Justification concerns roughly how to tell what's true, or, more precisely, how to judge a belief about what's true to be in various senses justified or unjustified.

14. More precisely, we cannot rely on anything that supports even one false belief *in the same way* that it supports true beliefs. But if we can meaningfully distinguish between some weak sort of support given to false beliefs and a stronger sort of support given only to true beliefs, then there is no problem.

15. In speaking of why we believe things, there are two distinct ideas in play. One is the idea of justification, concerning the reasons we have for thinking that a belief is true. The other idea concerns what caused us to hold a belief. These two different ideas point to the same referent in cases where someone arrives at a belief solely by reflecting on its justification. But usually the two referents are partly or wholly different. Each of the reasons for belief listed above can be a cause (or partial cause), a putative justification (or part of a putative justification), or both. Note that a belief can be caused by something that does not reliably lead to truth but then be vindicated by a justification that does reliably lead to truth. And note that where no adequate justification is offered for a belief, it's sensible to examine the causes of the belief as candidate justifications.

16. There will be readers who at this point want to speak of quantum mechanics. If a particle can be in two places at one time, doesn't this refute my statement above, and perhaps even refute the law of non-contradiction? No, it does not. Reality *is* some way, and *is not* any other way. If reality is such that a particle can be in two places at one time, then that's the way reality is, and reality is not any other way. Such a fact might overturn our prior notions about physics, but it does nothing to challenge the notions I've presented about reality and non-contradiction.

17. To implicitly believe proposition X means, in its simplest form, to

explicitly believe proposition Y when Y can only be true if X is true. Distinctions can be drawn between different degrees of implicit belief in X based on how many Ys depend upon X, how strongly those Ys are believed, and how central they are to a person's overall belief system. And we can consider how someone would respond if asked about X or shown one's logical commitment to X. But even vehement and sustained denial of X doesn't change X's status as an implicit belief if belief in Y persists.

18. This is another form of implicit belief, in which to implicitly believe proposition X means to act as if X were true.

19. We're committed to the truth of all our beliefs, but certainly not of all our statements. Lying is the simplest counterexample. There are also countless ways that statements can look like expressions of belief on the surface but upon further scrutiny prove to be more about expressing identity, signaling attitudes, or inspiring particular reactions, often with little interest in truth.

20. It is, of course, possible to care about truth in some areas but not others. But generally those areas in which ignoring truth might prove attractive or useful are precisely those areas in which ignoring truth leads to the absurdities above.

21. Or, we find ourselves thinking or saying that the contradiction is not problematic. But the inadequacy of this response should be clear from what's already been said.

22. By calling a worldview true I mean, to a first approximation, that all its constituent beliefs are true. But I do not mean that it fully describes reality, or even that it captures all or most of the true beliefs that could in principle be arrived at from the epistemic situation in which the worldview exists.

23. This is not to suggest that the two worldviews must be similarly robust or ambitious. One of them might be humbler and more agnostic, and in this sense its burdens may be lighter. But it can still fairly be seen as an entire worldview, fully responsible for whatever claims it does in fact entail.

## Chapter 2

# Evidence

We've seen that if we begin seeking to harmonize our beliefs and match them to reality we are driven toward issues of justification. And we've seen that although most sorts of justification offer equal support to contradictory views there seems to be one exception, namely methodical examination of the world and careful reasoning about what such examination finds. The usual term for this is science.

Some scientific inquiries concern things that can be rigorously tested under consistent conditions. Things like chemical reactions or the movements of falling objects can be tested over and over, by scientists around the world, in conditions that prevent extraneous influences.

But extraneous influences are harder to avoid in most scientific inquiries. When something occurs inside a cell or a rat or a human, it occurs within an extremely complex system, and instances of that system will vary in numerous ways, making it difficult to isolate any one variable and determine its effects. Scientists overcome this difficulty through what are known as controlled experiments, in which two groups have the same sorts of internal variations, and one group is exposed to the experimental variable while the other is not.

But sometimes a controlled experiment would involve decades of observation, billions of dollars in unavailable funding, or unacceptable harm to human subjects. Sometimes an experiment would involve manipulating stars or black holes or tectonic plates, which at present we could not do no matter how badly we wanted to. Some inquiries lie at the frontier of current scientific knowledge so that we don't know what we don't know, including what confounding variables might be involved. Some inquiries concern processes that occur over thousands or millions of years so that we cannot watch them occur, while some inquiries involve the particularity of how processes or events actually played out in the past, and not only how they can play out in principle.

Scientists meet these daunting challenges in ingenious ways. For example, sometimes controlled experiments are impossible but scientists are able to identify natural experiments that create comparable conditions. Examples include identical twins who are adopted by different families, employment in a metropolitan area spanning one U.S. state that raises its minimum wage and one that doesn't, and radiation exposure around Hiroshima and Nagasaki but not around other Japanese cities.

In scientific inquiries like physics and physical cosmology, many theories cannot be tested in simple or obvious ways, but scientists are able to tease out subtle implications of those theories and compare them with stunningly precise measurements of cosmic radiation, distant stars, or miniscule particles.

Often challenges encountered by one scientific inquiry are overcome using resources from other scientific inquiries. For example, entire civilizations rose and fell without leaving any written records, but scientists can dig through their ruins and their trash heaps, test the isotopes in their skeletons and the food debris in their dental plaque, take sediment cores from their lakes and analyze the layers of pollen, ash, and soil found there—and arrive at remarkably detailed pictures of how people in those civilizations lived and died. As another example, we've only recently begun recording the earth's climate, but scientists are able to learn about earlier climates from the oxygen isotopes incorporated into the shells of long-dead molluscs and crustaceans; the annual variations in tree growth rings going back thousands of years; the density of pores on fossilized leaves; and the contents of cores drilled from ice sheets, capturing snow that fell hundreds of thousands of years ago, with its differing isotope ratios reflecting differing temperatures when the snow fell, and with tiny pockets of ancient air trapped when the snow fell, and traces of atmospheric dust and volcanic ash in that air. As one more example, we weren't around for most of the history of life on earth, but scientists have pieced together a remarkable amount of that history from the scattered bits that fossilized, gathering and analyzing them with painstaking care, and drawing on what other scientists have learned about how organisms live and reproduce, how they change over generations, and what their anatomy and DNA reveal about their kinships and histories.

This complementary and interlocking character of scientific findings is one of the things that most strongly commend those findings to us. It suggests that the different ways in which different scientists study different parts of reality are succeeding, and converging from different angles on the same reality. And note that all these findings rest directly on observation. What can be seen through a telescope or microscope is just as real as what is seen with the naked eye. This basic dynamic holds no matter how sophisticated the instruments or experiments become. You can always in principle simply look for yourself.

And perhaps most compellingly, consider what the findings of science enable us to do. We carry supercomputers in our pockets that send sounds and pictures through the air invisibly, with some then beamed through hair-width fibers of super-clear glass that we've bundled and laid across continents and oceans, and some relayed by satellites we've launched into space to orbit our planet. We drive vehicles that create thousands of controlled explosions per minute and harness the energy of those explosions to move big boxes of metal and plastic that in the split-second while a crash is occurring can detect the crash and cause a chemical reaction that creates gas that fills a bag that saves a life. We take crash victims to hospitals where we use sound, magnetism, radiation, and antimatter to see inside bodies, and use molecules we've manufactured to kill bacteria, disrupt viruses, mute pain, and alter the functioning of cells and organs. We split atoms to release enormous energy that can power cities, or can release even more enormous energy through fusion and destroy cities, or can power submarines that stay underwater for months while extracting both oxygen and freshwater from surrounding seawater and carrying missiles that can be launched underwater, fly into space, reenter earth's atmosphere, and then destroy cities.

We don't have full mastery of the natural world, but the mastery that we do have is astounding, and it shapes every facet of contemporary life. From consumer products to medical care to apocalyptic weapons and much more, the contemporary world rests upon foundations of science.

Taken together, these points make a powerful case for the reliability of scientific findings. Indeed they lead many people to place complete trust in science. But others ask questions. How confidently can we embrace present scientific findings when so many prior scientific findings have in time been overturned? Can scientists ever be justified in moving from their limited observations to their universal theories? Do scientists' theories inevitably skew their observations? How is science affected by psychological, social, political, and economic forces? Do some disciplines wrongly co-opt the success or authority of other disciplines? Are scientists perhaps just another social group, with particular biases and interests, conducting what's merely one discourse among many? Does science give us powers we should not wield, like those involved in cloning, planet-warming engines, or city-destroying bombs? Does science alienate us from nature or from ourselves, undermining our traditional beliefs and ways of life?

We can begin by separating out some of these questions as practical or moral rather than epistemic. Concerns about playing God, creating godlike weapons, or undermining traditional belief in God could all be completely legitimate and correct without suggesting that science tells us anything false about the world. Important questions can be asked about the costs and risks of science, but our present question is merely whether science gathers reliable evidence about reality.

Next we can separate out questions that are relevant to the philosophy of science as an academic discipline but not to the sort of practical philosophy that this book is pursuing. Remember that we've already reckoned with the impossibility of certainty, and our notion of truth is provisional and approximate, and we are weighing competing sorts of justification against one another rather than against unattainable certainties. This allows us to embrace science without seeing it as perfect or complete, and without settling some of the thornier issues within the philosophy of science.

Three important issues remain. First, what are the boundaries of science? Is economics, for example, a science? Is the work of a cultural anthropologist as scientific as that of a chemist? Does every natural and social science, and every school of thought within each, deserve the same halo of credibility, or are there gradations or exclusions?

The answers to such questions are relatively simple in principle, and are implicit in what's already been said. Across disciplines and contexts, all of science is characterized by methodical examination of the world and careful reasoning about what's found through such examination. It is this general approach, rather than the objects of study or the labels of disciplines, that makes an inquiry scientific. And the way to judge whether a scientific inquiry is succeeding, and gaining reliable evidence about reality, is by the considerations discussed above: whether the findings rest ultimately on observation, so that in principle you could simply look for yourself; whether the findings interlock with the findings of other scientists and other disciplines; and whether the findings give us the ability to manipulate parts of reality that we were unable to manipulate before, or, similarly, to predict things that we were unable to predict before. These are the general criteria we can use to judge whether any given discipline or school of thought or body of work is or is not scientific. Making particular judgments may still be difficult or contentious, but the principles for judging seem straightforward.

The next important issue is how science might be skewed or corrupted by psychological, social, political, and economic forces. How are individual scientists affected by our normal human weaknesses of thought? How easily can their work be skewed by their funding, their beliefs, their feelings, or their social groups? And how can this be intentionally manipulated by powerful actors in industry, government, or elsewhere?

These are not new challenges that hit science from the outside. Instead these challenges help to motivate and structure science from the start. The idea is not that scientists are super-human individuals who lack our usual weaknesses, but rather that those weaknesses can be overcome through the structures of scientific practice. The idea is not that an isolated scientist can be brilliant enough to think without errors, but that scientists work and cooperate and compete in ways designed to expose and correct errors. At every turn, fellow scientists demand evidence, scrutinize methods, and make counterarguments. And there are deep social and professional norms of skepticism, conservatism, and, above all, attention to evidence.

This is not to say that these structures always work perfectly, because they don't. But when an armchair critic finds fault with experimental methods or guesses at alternate explanations for data, the odds are very good that it's the critic who is mistaken. For while the scientists remain fallible, they have already worked very hard and very intentionally to do things like consider all alternate explanations, identify all confounding variables, scrutinize all procedures and equipment, and judge by hard statistics over mere intuitions.

But what about when some potential influence pushes on many scientists, and pushes them all in the same direction? Can this perhaps overcome science's usual defenses? If a given assumption were strong enough in enough scientists, then might it be able to slip past the usual rigor and skepticism of relevant gatekeepers? Or if something false has made its way into the current scientific consensus, then might the conservatism that usually prevents new errors instead serve to preserve an old error? And what about the salaries and research funding offered by businesses, universities, governments, and other institutions? How might this lead scientists to serve the beliefs, values, and interests of the individuals behind the money? And what levels of influence might be achieved by direct or indirect enticement or coercion from the most powerful individuals or institutions?

These dangers are very real. But let's consider what sorts of inferences they do and do not support. Toward one end of the spectrum, imagine if there were a scientific issue that was very important to some powerful industry, and that industry funded research and publishing on the issue that supported a position favorable to the industry, while all the other scientists working on the issue and receiving their funding from a wide range of public and private sources around the world agreed on a different position that was unfavorable to the industry. Something like this would strongly suggest that the industry-backed scientists were being improperly influenced, and their work did not offer reliable evidence about reality. Such a situation would seem to support the rejection of some scientific findings, namely those of the industry-backed scientists, in favor of the competing findings of the other scientists.

But as we move away from scenarios as glaring as that one the prospect of rejecting scientific findings becomes much more daunting. I grant that in absolutely any case it is possible to doubt an individual scientist's motives or choices or skills.

And in absolutely any case it is possible to ask about subtle personal, social, professional, or ideological influences, or about clandestine bribes or threats. But note that such doubts or questions do not stand alone; they are parts of a larger whole, namely the entire worldview or set of worldviews with which they are consistent. So if you poke holes in some particular experiment or theory or discipline, you are not only engaged in poking those holes, but also in the implicit assertion of some worldview that fits with such hole-poking.

For example imagine that you want to reject some particular scientific theory that scientists generally accept. In doing so, you suggest that hundreds of scientists around the world, working in different settings and funded through different channels, are all fabricating or misinterpreting the evidence they cite. And to explain why this is so, you either suggest that the sorts of causes I've mentioned above happen to affect every one of those scientists and to lead each of them to the same false conclusion, or else you suggest some sort of coordinated conspiracy.

Every part of your view falls within the wide realm of logical possibility. And given the evidence we have about the world, there are probably few if any parts of your view that I could decisively disprove.[24] So if you wanted to just adhere to your view, and insist that it could be true and has not been disproven, you could do so. But notice that this is not the same as showing that your view is true, or is at all likely to be true. When you try to show such things you'll quickly tie yourself into the knot of being demanding and skeptical toward the arguments of the preceding pages while being exceedingly gentle and credulous toward your own arguments for a conspiracy. You will be demanding certainty from my arguments while accepting your own because of mere possibility or suspicion. And that's not a very tenable position.

One psychological pitfall here is that our minds rely far too much on mere coherence. If some view, such as an unfounded view about a grand conspiracy, seems coherent, then that fact alone inclines us to give it serious attention, or even to embrace it as true. But as noted earlier, it's possible to fabricate countless views that are coherent but bear little resemblance to reality.

These points admittedly do not fully vindicate any scientific theory or fully disprove any conspiracy theory. Nor do they draw any bright line between untenable conspiracy theories and scenarios that really do suggest improper outside influences on science. But they do establish the general soundness of the scientific enterprise, and the general skepticism that's deserved by arguments against any particular scientific findings.

The final issue we need to address is the very practical issue of how to navigate everything we're told about science, whether from peer-reviewed scientific journals, other technical works, popularizations by scientists or journalists, other journalistic works, documentaries, encyclopedias, textbooks, or teachers. How closely do each of these sources reflect the scientific findings we've been speaking of?

In terms of gathering evidence, scientific findings are found in the laboratory or out in the field. But in terms of understanding and interpreting this evidence, scientific findings generally emerge from the ongoing process of publication and criticism within a community of specialists. A new discovery is made and published, and then ruthlessly attacked by specialists in the field, and if it manages to survive scrutiny and get corroborated by additional work, then it may slowly gain acceptance within the specialty. If that acceptance grows into a consensus among the specialists, then that consensus is the sort of scientific finding we've been considering. That is where we can be most confident that we have reliable scientific evidence about reality. This is the wellspring from which scientific knowledge flows.

But there's substantial distance between this scientific consensus, as it exists within each of hundreds of communities of specialists, and the individual who is trying to make sense of the world and live in it. How can an individual learn about that scientific consensus, or at least about whatever parts of it are philosophically relevant, without needing to master each specialty and join each community of specialists? We'll briefly examine the most common paths.

For most people scientific knowledge begins in earnest as a part of formal education, through the instruction of teachers and the textbooks that guide it. Advanced textbooks reflect the scientific consensus of specialists quite directly, after a short time lag. So when such books are used by competent instructors, students gain scientific knowledge that's highly reliable and close to its source.

But the competence of instructors is not a given, so this constitutes one important caveat. And there are two others, each of which grows more pressing as we move toward textbooks and instruction at lower levels. First, with minors, and especially with younger minors, and especially in certain social contexts, there can be pressures from parents or outside groups to omit or downplay disfavored parts of the scientific consensus, usually meaning parts of biology that are taken to contradict religious dogma or to support disfavored political views. The last caveat concerns summarizing and simplifying. An advanced textbook for graduate students can reproduce the content of the scientific consensus just as it exists in the minds of specialists. But this won't do for a high school textbook, let alone an elementary one. So material must be summarized and simplified, which raises difficult questions about what points have what intellectual or practical relevance.

Wherever one's science education leaves off or gets forgotten, one can go directly to the advanced textbooks. But there are less strenuous alternatives, from encyclopedias to documentaries to news articles to popular science books. But caution is needed, because some of these sources are actually a result of scientific ignorance rather than a solution to it. One prominent example is news articles that address a single study of the health effects of some food or drink or exercise and herald the results as if they were a settled scientific consensus. This fails to give readers accurate information, and it also does positive damage by making many laymen think that scientific findings change constantly, and if scientists thought that coffee was healthy last week but think it's unhealthy this week, for example, then are they really so sure about other things? In addition, news reports often herald new discoveries without saying much about how the discoveries were made or how they relate to what was already known. Another example is the occasional medical doctor who writes books or appears on television to promote some unfounded pet theory or fad diet, presenting himself as a scientific authority while ignoring all his scientific training. A final example is nature documentaries that aggressively anthropomorphize their animal subjects, and lead viewers to simply project our human emotions and deliberations instead of learning anything about animal cognition and behavior.[25]

But many documentaries, popularizations, encyclopedias, and journalistic works are excellent, and faithfully convey scientific knowledge in ways that are accessible and engaging. So the question is how to distinguish the good from the bad. While you are in the process of learning this is of course difficult to judge directly. But you can look to indirect indicators, such as the reputation of a journalist or journalistic outlet, or the way the popularizing work of a journalist or scientist is regarded by relevant specialists. And the more scientific knowledge you gain, the more you can begin to judge, at least provisionally, how much any given claim is also supported by other sources, and how well it comports with other relevant claims that are widely accepted.

---

24. This is largely because of the difficulty of proving a negative. It is, for example, easy to prove that there are wild pandas in China, but

almost impossible to prove that there are none in Mexico. It is in most cases similarly difficult to prove the absence of conspiracies.

25. This is especially unfortunate because learning about animal impulses and reactions can shed light on our own psychology, whereas if we merely cling to our prereflective impressions of ourselves and project them onto animals, this can hold us back from understanding either one.

# Chapter 3

# Belief

We've now established the basics of our epistemic situation. We started from scratch, which is a common impulse in philosophy, and which certainly has its virtues. But this impulse runs up against the facts that no one actually does start from scratch, and that even when we're reasoning about foundational matters we're also holding views about matters built on top of those foundations.[26] And while logically speaking the foundations should determine what can be built on top, the opposite often occurs, as we instead choose foundations in order to support conclusions we like.

In the case of this book, we started with relatively narrow epistemic questions, but the further we pursue them the more they shape, and are shaped by, some broader picture of what we are and how our minds work. Evaluating such pictures involves consulting the scientific findings discussed in the last chapter. But it also requires addressing claims that complement or compete with those findings, especially claims rooted in religion.

That single term "religion" is used for an immense range of ideas and actions, on scales from the individual to the great cultural and political forces of history. But our focus in discussing religion will be on religious claims, meaning the propositional claims that emerge from all this, or that provide its intellectual support. In the end we'll conclude that we lack adequate reason to embrace any religious claims. But we'll also see that this conclusion isn't as easy or tidy as some people imagine.

\* \* \*

In the preceding chapters it was fairly straightforward to embrace reason and evidence in principle. But things get harder in practice, as reason and evidence sometimes lead toward conclusions that conflict with our natural inclinations. Such conflicts can be addressed individually, but they also give rise to general questions of how much trust we should place in those natural inclinations—and these are the questions that lead us to examine religious claims. For if some broadly religious account of reality is true, and there is, for example, a God who designed our minds and our world, then it might be reasonable to generally trust our minds, follow our intuitions, and expect the world to make sense to us. But things look very different if instead we are, for example, products of unguided evolution, with minds shaped only for their tendency to aid survival and reproduction in particular environments. In that case it might be reasonable to distrust our minds, question our intuitions, and expect parts of the world to baffle us.

In turning our attention to religion, our task is to take the epistemic agreement around reason and evidence built in the preceding chapters and use it to build as much agreement as possible on religious matters.[27] For across religious traditions and all varieties of nonreligious thought, few people are willing to repudiate reason or evidence. And it turns out that the epistemic basics on which we agree are adequate to answer many of the religious questions on which we so wildly and stubbornly disagree.[28]

In moving out from the safety of epistemic agreement into the peril of religious disagreement, we will focus on foundations. We will not, for example, begin with some soaring judgment that religion is good or bad for society, because that would involve incredibly complex issues of analyzing religious phenomena, analyzing entire societies, and normatively evaluating what's good or bad for a society, all of which involve enormous challenges of their own. Instead we'll focus on foundational religious arguments, such as arguments either for or against the existence of God, the existence of a soul, or the truth of a particular religion. And we'll examine such arguments using only the epistemic basics that we've already established, assuming nothing further, no matter how commonsensical it might seem or how easy it might be to smuggle in.

One thing this means is making no assumptions about what these religious arguments must look like. Religious arguments will be met on their own terms, with openness to any form of justification that might be offered. Doing otherwise simply wouldn't be justified. For while we've seen that careful, explicit reasoning leads toward truth, we have *not* seen that it's the *only* thing that does. And likewise we've seen that science gives us reliable evidence about reality, but we have *not* seen that it's the *only* thing that does. When opponents of religion claim that religious belief could be justified only by conclusive rational proofs or clear scientific evidence, they are mistaken. Such claims might sound plausible in light of cultural attitudes toward reason and science, but they are not rationally justified. If there is in fact a God or some other spiritual reality, then whatever its attitudes may be, we are not remotely justified in assuming that they match ours. Perhaps if you were God you would make your existence scientifically demonstrable. That's fine. But it has no relevance here.

While opening the doors to all types of arguments in this way, there is just one demand we can make, and must make. This demand is that for anything to count as supporting a belief it must support that belief more strongly than it supports any contradictory belief, and for anything to count as supporting a course of action it must support that course of action more strongly than it supports any alternative course of action. Because we are surrounded by a vast number of religious and irreligious views, all screaming their contradictory claims and demands, and we need a reason to move in one direction rather than any other. Anything that pulls us in multiple directions cannot help us decide, and anything that pulls us toward contradictory claims must be pulling us toward falsehoods. Such things leave us frozen while the screaming continues on all sides.

Some of the screams consist of religious justifications that say the path to religion runs not through reason and evidence but through intuition, or feelings of love, or following supernatural guidance, or choosing in the face of uncertainty. We'll see later that such ideas can be parts of broader justifications that have substantial merit. But it's another matter when they are offered as full justifications in themselves. In that case they run afoul of our sole requirement and give equal support to contradictory beliefs and contrary courses of action.[29]

Looking narrowly, there is nothing irrational or otherwise problematic about someone embracing Sunni Islam, for example, because of strong intuitions, or feelings of love or reverence for God, or experiences of divine guidance, or conscious choice in the face of uncertainty. But the problem is that for identical reasons others embrace Evangelical Christianity while others join Catholic monasteries while others pursue purely personal spiritualities. So when these sorts of justifications stand alone, they get us nowhere.

But what if all those spiritual responses are equally good while a total absence of spirituality is bad? That's logically possible. But do we have reason to think it's actually true? It faces the same challenges as other attempts to affirm points of agreement among religions—like areas of moral agreement or stances of gratitude or reverence—without embracing the religions themselves. Appreciating the difficulty requires that we step back and note some general features of religious epistemologies.

Some religious individuals and groups are not especially transparent about the epistemic bases of what they believe to be true. An example of this would be growing up hearing and embracing stories about gods or spirits but never hearing much about where those stories came from. But most forms of religion are not like this, and instead involve prominent attributions of some or all of their doctrines to sacred texts, teachers, or institutions, which are understood either as a matter of holy or wise individuals managing to gain special insight into spiritual realities or as a matter of some spiritual reality actively revealing itself. The result is a body of teachings that are taken to be true because of their special provenance.

Sometimes this is explicit and emphatic, as when a religious group states directly and frequently that its claims are true because they come from a sacred text that came from God. But even when that's not the case, important claims are still made which would not be made if not for the body of teachings thought to have a special provenance, and which would cease to be made if those teachings were rejected.[30] So such religious claims depend upon a religion's sacred texts, teachers, or institutions, whether or not such dependence is a frequent talking point.[31]

Now let's imagine three different justifications for the claim that murder is wrong,[32] one based on Buddha's wisdom and enlightenment, another based on Allah's revelation to his prophet Muhammad, and another based on the scripture and tradition entrusted to the Roman Catholic Church. If you accept any one of those religious foundations, then you have a religious justification for the claim that murder is wrong. But if you don't accept any of those religious foundations then you don't have any of the justifications based on them. And the mere fact that those different justifications support the same claim is not itself a justification.

Perhaps the claim that murder is wrong can be justified on different grounds altogether, depending on neither the Buddha nor the Quran nor the Church. But if so then the justification depends on precisely those grounds, whatever they are, and not on the fact that the religious justifications happen to agree.[33] In the same way, a Buddhist can make various arguments for the goodness of her spirituality that are based on Buddha's insight, while a Muslim can make arguments for the goodness of her spirituality based on Muhammad's revelation, and a Catholic can make arguments for the goodness of her spirituality based on the Church's authority—but someone who does not accept any of those religious foundations cannot make any of those arguments.[34]

So as a general matter, if we are to affirm any point of agreement among religions, we'll need a reason beyond the mere fact of that agreement. And in the particular matter of religious justifications like raw intuition or choice, which give equal support to contradictory claims and divergent paths, such justifications get us nowhere. So we must now look elsewhere, and begin examining more substantive sorts of religious arguments. The process will be long, but once we finish we'll be in a position to weigh up all the relevant arguments and evidence together, and judge where they point.

\* \* \*

There are arguments about the existence of souls, and the existence of God, and whether particular accounts of God are internally consistent or consistent with the world we observe. There are arguments for and against particular religious traditions, sects, institutions, texts, and teachers. And there are arguments about what presumptions we should start with, which standards to apply to which arguments, and how to respond to uncertainty.

There are arguments that there must be a God who created our world; that there must be a God who was the first cause of all the effects that we observe; that features of living organisms, or of the planet and cosmos that make them possible, must have been designed by a God; that our conscious experience cannot be explained by our brains and this shows that we are immortal souls who will live on in other bodies or in an afterlife; that for the pain and injustice of life to make sense there must be a divine plan or cosmic reckoning; that if we're uncertain whether there is a God then we should believe just to be safe; that we should err on the side of being religious because religion tends to make people happier and more moral; that, in contrast, religion tends to support cruelty and ignorance, and should be rejected; that religion is an artifact of the past that is no longer needed and no longer useful; that religions are failed attempts to explain what can now be explained scientifically; that the pain and injustice of life show that no God exists; and many more.

We'll begin working our way through these arguments by examining the aspects of reality that they cluster around. This will require you to do several difficult things. First take note of the conclusions about religion that you personally bring into this inquiry, whatever they are. Because even though we're progressing toward conclusions, most readers already have their own conclusions in mind. And we have a natural loyalty to our conclusions. But because we are equally loyal to contradictory conclusions, some of that loyalty must be misplaced. And even if we were to assume that all of your particular conclusions are true, it would still be the case that there are weak arguments for true conclusions and strong arguments for false conclusions. Similarly, unreliable evidence gets cited in support of true conclusions while reliable evidence gets cited in support of false ones. And what all this means is that it's essential to separate your conclusions from the arguments and evidence that support them, and not identify them too closely in your mind.

We naturally embrace whatever seems to support our conclusions and naturally reject whatever seems to oppose them, but this is foolish. Inasmuch as we want to be rational, and to see reality clearly, we need to work against these natural tendencies.

We need to strain to see weaknesses in our own arguments and evidence, and strain to see strengths in opposing arguments and evidence. And we can do this secure in the knowledge that a conclusion does not stand and fall with every single argument or piece of evidence. You can admit a weakness in an argument for your conclusion without abandoning the conclusion. And you can admit that one of your opponent's arguments is strong without accepting his conclusion.

This requires discipline, and it can be emotionally difficult, but rationally it's quite simple. Judge arguments and evidence by their merits, not by whether they point toward what you already think. And realize that for every dispute between a truth and a falsehood, there are both good and bad arguments on both sides, drawing on both reliable and unreliable evidence.

But while you should see a conclusion as independent of a particular argument for it, you should *not* see it as independent of *all* arguments for it. This can be a delicate balance. On the one hand, hold your conclusion steady so that you can calmly and fairly evaluate its supporting arguments on their own merits. But on the other hand, don't hold your conclusion steady forever. Realize that if argument after argument for some conclusion turns out to be weak while argument after argument against it turns out to be strong, then at some point you'll need to reevaluate the conclusion. Or at least you'll need to do so if you want to maintain any claims to being rational and believing true things.

With these points in mind let's begin working our way through the arguments, starting with matters of cosmology and biology. These matters involve some disputes about evidence, but the resolution to most of these disputes is clear. The preceding two chapters started from scratch and built an account of how to grope our way toward truth. This account involved embracing science as a way to gather reliable evidence about reality. And scientists have gathered reliable evidence about how the physical universe began and developed, and how life on earth began and developed. This evidence does not answer all questions, and as we will see it does not dictate answers to our present religious questions. But as far as it goes, addressing the basic facts of life and cosmology, the scientific evidence is clear. For many decades now it has not been in doubt, and has only grown more solid and more extensive. So we will follow the reasoning of the preceding chapters and accept these findings of science about the basic facts. For a reader to do otherwise because these facts seem to oppose some of his conclusions would be for that reader to abandon our project of rationality and truth. Because his conclusions are precisely what we're now trying to reason about. And to preemptively reject evidence because you think it hurts your conclusions is to turn away from reality and instead pursue pleasant dreams.

The evidence about physical cosmology shows that roughly 13.8 billion years ago matter, energy, space, and time exploded into existence. Physical processes then played out on massive scales for massive spans of time, resulting in the first stars after 700 million years, and after another 8.5 billion years resulting in the star that is our sun, and the planets that orbit it.

That initial explosion is known as the Big Bang, and we do not know what caused it, or whether asking about its cause even makes sense. Some physicists offer speculative accounts of why the Big Bang occurred, or was perhaps even bound to occur, but these are speculations without hard evidence, and at best they offer explanatory possibilities.

Other possibilities are not physical but metaphysical, not natural but supernatural. Some spiritual being could have created the material universe; some eternal being could have created time; some first cause or unmoved mover could lie behind all effects and all movement. In this sense our scientific knowledge can be seen as giving support to religion. But at the same time, no ancient religious account of creation bears an especially striking resemblance to the Big Bang. And whatever support religion gets here, whether rooted more in scientific Big Bang cosmology or in philosophical arguments about causation or metaphysics, this support only points toward a bare cause, and on its own it gets us nowhere near the full-blooded Gods of religion.

Turning to biology, the evidence shows that organisms are built on DNA blueprints, and they pass on their DNA to their offspring. Whenever a small change in a DNA blueprint creates an organism that's slightly better at surviving and reproducing in its environment, that DNA gets passed on to that organism's more numerous offspring. And over very long spans of time, these small changes add up to all the variety that we observe.

The core of Darwinian evolution[35] is as simple as that, and is a matter of emphatic agreement among scientists. The evidence of paleontology, anatomy, and genetics is overwhelming, ranging from the subtle and technical to things as glaring as the vestigial hind leg bones that whales have inside them, or the homology among tetrapod limbs from the whale's flipper to the dog's paw to the bat's wing to the human hand. And evolution has extensive practical applications in medicine, agriculture, ecology, and elsewhere. Few things in science are better-attested or more central to scientific theory and practice than evolution.

The facts of evolution conflict with particular creation stories, but the connection to general religious questions is more attenuated. If you believe that evolution adequately explains living things, then you can stop there and say nothing theological, or you can claim that there is a God behind evolution, or you can claim that there's no God behind it. And if you believe that evolution does not adequately explain living things, then you can stop there and say nothing theological, or you can claim that there's no God, or you can claim that there is a God and whatever is not adequately explained by evolution is instead explained by this God. So at this level, matters of God and matters of evolution are mostly separate, with the possible exception that there may be things that cannot be explained by evolution but can be explained by God.

But that sort of move—attributing something that we cannot explain to God, and even citing it as evidence for God's existence—is rather shaky. Because as science has progressed, over and over some gap in scientific knowledge has been cited as evidence for the existence of God, only for that gap to be filled in by later scientific work. This suggests that we should be slow to draw conclusions from any current gaps. And even if such conclusions can be drawn, they will be subject to the same sorts of qualifications noted for cosmology, namely that even if we could infer a supernatural cause behind some particular evolutionary event this would not especially resemble the stories told by any religions,[36] and the cause we could infer would still be miles from the Gods of religion, albeit getting closer, in ways we'll explore in a moment.

Arguments that evolution cannot adequately explain life take several forms. Some focus on particular transitions in the fossil record and claim that they represent gulfs that could not have been crossed by unguided evolution, and therefore a God must have been involved. But these arguments are the less promising sort, for several reasons. First, they reject the judgments of virtually all paleontologists, evolutionary biologists, and other specialists who professionally study such matters. Second, they often misunderstand the nature of the fossil record and speak as if somehow it should be a complete transcript of life's history, rather than the uneven smattering of clues that it actually is, composed of only those bits of life that ended under extremely unusual conditions and therefore fossilized. And third, such arguments often rely on our gut senses of time and probability, effectively insisting that a particular transition or a particular level of complexity just *feels* like it could not have come about through unguided evolution and its dependence on blind chance. But we must appreciate that if we did indeed come about through evolution, then so did those very senses of time and probability. This would mean that they came about to aid our survival and reproduction as animals that live several decades. And the judgments of time and probability that would serve that goal differ radically from those applicable to the eons of evolutionary time.

The more promising arguments that evolution is inadequate to explain life instead focus on life's beginning. Evolution as we know it depends upon the DNA blueprints of organisms, which are continually passed on with modifications, thereby enabling the evolutionary process to unfold across generations. But this DNA-dependent process cannot explain DNA itself. So some argue that a God must lie behind the creation of DNA, or more generally behind the creation of the first life forms, known as abiogenesis. These arguments have at least some merit, because while there are naturalistic theories of abiogenesis, none of them have yet been confirmed by conclusive evidence and become a scientific consensus.

But these arguments also face difficulties, beginning with the precarity of inferring God from a gap in present scientific knowledge. In addition, this particular gap is actually smaller than it might appear. Because while the DNA-based description of evolution above was simple, the central logic of evolution is even simpler. All that's required is self-replication. Once any self-replicating entity arises, evolution is off to the races, as there comes to be more of what makes more of itself. These self-replicating entities will eventually come into competition of some sort, and those that replicate more successfully will displace those that are less successful, leading to change over time. This is what happens with DNA-based replication, but DNA is not necessary, nor is anything similarly complex.[37]

Another sort of argument spans cosmology and biology and

notes that if there were even slight differences in the universe's fundamental physical laws or constants, or in how the Big Bang occurred, then life as we know it could not exist. The universe would have quickly collapsed back in upon itself, or it would have ballooned too quickly for stars and planets to ever form, or carbon atoms would not have been forged inside dying stars, or liquid water would not exist, etc. From this it's argued that the universe was finely tuned to allow for life, and the tuning was done by God.

This argument faces several difficulties. First are the limits of our knowledge of physics, which make it difficult to speak about which forces and constants actually could have differed, and how, and what would have resulted. But even if we grant that the laws and constants and the beginning of our universe could indeed have differed, so that our universe's suitability for life is indeed unlikely, other difficulties remain. One is that any particular set of laws, constants, and initial conditions would be unlikely, just as any particular set of lottery numbers or hand of bridge is unlikely, but this does not mean that the one unlikely alternative that actually occurs requires a special explanation. Another is that even if a life-supporting universe is in some senses surprising, in other senses it is not, because it's the only sort of universe we could find ourselves living in. We could never observe a universe that could not support observers. And lastly, it's possible that our universe is one among many, which could mean our particular laws and constants were bound to occur in one of them, which, again, would have to be the one we found ourselves in.

And we yet again encounter the issue of how close a cause or creator or fine-tuner would get us to the Gods of religion. I am not suggesting that arguments from cosmology or biology would need to prove some full theology of Brahman or Allah or the Trinity in order to succeed. But at the same time, if we grant a supernatural cause behind the Big Bang, for example, we would still have no reason to think that this cause is a God who wants us to live, believe, and worship in particular ways.

If we grant a supernatural creator of the first living organisms or a supernatural fine-tuner of the universe this would go a bit further, implying intelligence, intention, power, and some sort of interest in biological life, and in the case of a fine-tuner implying something outside our universe and with the power to determine it, at least initially. But still there would be no inkling that it had any ongoing involvement in the universe, or any interest in humans above other forms of life, or any concern for individual humans and how they live. And even if it did have such concern, it could just as well want us to be skeptical as to have faith, or to be atheists as to be religious, or to be cruel or selfish or debauched as to follow any religious morality. So these efforts at proving God's existence do not, on their own, give us any guidance on how to live or any reason to move toward religious belief.

* * *

Next we come to human consciousness—meaning roughly our subjective experience of being aware and unified selves who think and choose and act—and whether it can be fully explained by the human brain[38] or can only be explained with recourse to a soul.[39] This issue largely mirrors what we saw with evolution and creation. If you believe that the brain adequately explains consciousness, then you can stop there and say nothing theological, or you can claim that there is also a soul, or you can claim that there's no soul. While if you believe that the brain does *not* adequately explain consciousness, then you can stop there and say nothing theological, or you can claim that there's no soul, or you can claim that there is a soul and whatever is not adequately explained by the brain is instead explained by the soul. And here as with evolution, we should be wary of drawing conclusions from any gaps in present scientific knowledge, because such gaps have a long history of closing.

So can the brain adequately explain consciousness? The brain is enormously complex and not fully understood. But scientists have managed to unlock many of its secrets, from the incredible machinery of individual neurons to the specialization of different brain regions to the cooperation of numerous regions in performing specific tasks. But debate centers on whether all this complex functioning can give rise to our overall experience of being conscious.

The answer begins with smaller and less controversial things that we know about the brain. Extensive scientific work has shown that many of our simple mental experiences arise from massive underlying complexity. For example routine actions like walking, speaking, or recognizing a friend's face involve feats of neural computation and integration of which we have no conscious awareness. And some of our mental experiences actively diverge from what lies beneath, as is the case when we recall memories with total confidence, so that remembering feels like replaying a video, when in fact much of the remembered content is made up during the act of remembering, and memories are full of errors, omissions, and confabulations. In these cases it seems that our conscious experience is less like a direct reflection of what the brain is doing and more like a useful simulation emerging from it, giving us a simplified interface with a complex world.

The same could be true of consciousness as a whole. It could be that our experience of awareness and selfhood is simply how our brains translate and integrate all the complexity of their underlying processes. It could be that our conscious experiencing and acting is how our brains unify the outputs of many independent, and sometimes conflicting, mental processes, so that one body can take unified action in response to all its perceptions and all its impulses.

This sort of explanation could be true, but admittedly we don't know. But note that such a possibility is enough to deflate the argument that the brain *cannot* explain consciousness and therefore souls must exist. At the same time, though, this sort of explanation is no argument *against* souls existing. I've simply claimed that consciousness can be explained by the brain. That's not to say a soul couldn't be hanging around too.

The view of consciousness just sketched can also be used to address issues of free will, which are contentious in their own right, and are used to argue both for and against religious claims. These arguments start with our notions of moral responsibility, which generally seem to require free will, or with our subjective experience of feeling free, deliberating between alternatives, and choosing our beliefs and actions at least some of the time. It's argued that the sort of freedom that we seem to experience, or that's required by our notions of moral responsibility, is incompatible with a naturalistic picture in which consciousness is fully explained by the brain and the brain is fully explained by lawlike physical processes; or alternatively, it's argued that such freedom is incompatible with religious pictures in which God already knows what will happen in the future, or has actively predestined everything that will happen.

Regarding the subjective experience of having free will, the preceding account of consciousness applies directly. If conscious experience as a whole is a sort of simulation or fiction then so is the conscious experience of having free will. It could be useful and perhaps unavoidable but not truthful. The same can be said of our notions of moral responsibility. Perhaps it's true that we're never actually morally responsible in the ways we imagine, but also true that it's impossible or undesirable to think and act as if that's the case.

* * *

Other arguments for religion deal with meaning and morality, drawing on some of our very deepest feelings and values. These arguments can be formulated in various ways, but the most straightforward is to say that we share certain strong intuitions around matters of morality and matters of the significance or meaning of human life that could be supported by a variety of religious views in ways that they cannot be supported without any religious views. The notions of rightness, wrongness, and meaningfulness that can be rationally supported by a God or a cosmic moral order bear a resemblance to one another and to our intuitions around such matters, but no comparable notions can be similarly supported by the material universe alone. This can be shown best by sketching the notions rationally supported by a particular religious account and then comparing them with what's supported by other religious accounts and what's supported by a thoroughly nonreligious account.

So consider the traditional theistic[40] account that in the beginning was God. God is prior to and independent of absolutely everything else. The causal and explanatory bedrock of everything is not the universe or matter or physics but God. And God is all-powerful and totally unconstrained. God then freely chooses to create the entire physical universe, and to create humans within it. And God values humanity, and cares about individual humans, and commands some things and forbids others. And after humans die God judges them, and gives rewards and punishments that last through eternity.

An account like this sees meaning and morals at the core of reality. It casts the entire universe as a product of intention and valuing, and human life as especially so. And central to human life is a robust morality, with some things being deeply and emphatically right and others being deeply and emphatically wrong. Such rightness and wrongness are rooted in the will of God, which is on this account the highest possible standard and deepest possible foundation, and is the same place where life's value or purpose or meaningfulness is rooted. Human life is valuable because God values it, and made it to resemble and relate to him. And humans have a purpose, a calling, to relate to God, to live morally, and simply to live the life God's given in the world God's created. In such purpose and in such morality there is a profound sort of obligation to honor and obey the God who fully merits it, and to thank the God to whom everything is owed, and to fear the God who gives eternal rewards and punishments, which rewards and punishments will put right all the apparent tragedy and injustice of this world.

Some see it as cheating to trace everything to God in this way. But such an account is logically possible, and we're presently entertaining the prospect that it's true. In that case the account would not be cheating by, for example, invoking God ad hoc to solve every intellectual problem that arises; it would be acknowledging the truth that everything does in fact arise from God. It would be no different in principle from rooting everything in the material universe if that is in fact where everything is rooted.[41]

Some object in particular to the view that what's right is right because God commands it, rather than God commanding it because it's right, with a central worry being that in that case morality would be arbitrary, and its content could have been radically different if God's commands had been different. Debate around this issue, known as the Euthyphro dilemma, is partly irrelevant for our purposes, and will be partly addressed by the very points we're working toward, but there are two underappreciated points that can be made right now.

First, if the God of traditional theism exists and morality is determined by his will, this might involve arbitrariness of a certain sort, but not the sort that's sometimes alleged. It would not, for example, be like some average Joe having the power to determine right and wrong, and to potentially turn morality on its head while all else remained unchanged. It is instead a radical picture of all things flowing from God, and God decreeing moral laws as well as physical laws and perhaps even logical laws. It is a picture of God's will determining not only what's right and wrong, but also the very nature and existence of the entire universe in which rightness and wrongness and humans exist in the first place.[42]

Second, this picture of God creating all things involves God creating our minds. God created us the way he did, and that's why we think and feel as we do, whereas if he'd created us differently then we'd think and feel differently. And this has potent consequences for the Euthyphro dilemma. As things stand we recoil from the wrongness of murder, for example, and some argue against God determining morality because it seems to entail that God could command murder instead of forbidding it, and that would make murder morally right, and would make for an evil or absurd world, or an evil God instead of the righteous God of traditional theism. But this all takes its force from our present feelings about murder. What if God had commanded murder and had also created us to feel that murder is right? That's hard for us to imagine, granted, but if it had actually occurred it would be equally hard for us to imagine otherwise. In fact, in that alternate scenario we might expect to find murderous ethicists considering the Euthyphro dilemma, and some opposing the idea that what's right is right because God commands it since then God could command something crazy, something that we all *know* is wrong—God could even command people *not to murder!*

\* \* \*

When we speak of the meaning of life, whether of an individual life or of all human life or of only certain lives or aspects of lives, there are three interrelated but distinct ideas in play. First is the idea of individuals making sense or making meaning. This involves finding life intelligible or creating some coherent story about it. Second is the idea of life having some sort of intrinsic meaning, significance, purpose, or value. Third is individuals' perceptions, feelings, or beliefs about such intrinsic meaning, significance, purpose, or value. So the first and third ideas concern what goes on inside someone's head, while the second idea concerns some quality or property that life actually has, or fails to have; it concerns the actual meaning, significance, purpose, or value of human life, as it truly is, independent of our correct or incorrect beliefs about it.

There are many conceptions of what life's meaning is, but our present concern is not with this question but rather with the meaningfulness itself. We are asking not what is meaningful but what meaningfulness is. This question is not addressed by the competing claims that the meaning of life is, for example, to be happy, to come to know God, to create a better world, or to pass on your genes. We're instead focused on how any such prescription is built into reality through the intention or valuing of a God, or through whatever else might prove comparable.

Having addressed these initial points, we can consider the notions of morality and meaningfulness that are rationally supported by traditional theism, and consider how they compare with our intuitions, with what's supported by other religious views, and with what's supported by thoroughly nonreligious views.

On the theistic picture rightness, wrongness, and meaning are utterly real and important, and are rooted directly in God, which is the deepest foundation and highest standard possible. This emphatic realness is essentially the same under other religious accounts. Whether rooted in the totally free will of God, or in features of God's nature or character,[43] or in Eastern notions of a cosmic moral order in which God is impersonal or even absent, morality and meaning are exceedingly solid and definite features of reality.

And broadly speaking this matches our intuitions. Consider the worth of the life of your child, your mother, your closest friend. Consider the labors of whatever humanitarian, martyr, leader, or rebel you find most moving. Consider the wrongness of the most awful crimes like rape, or bombing neighborhoods, or torturing innocents. Consider the rightness of the noblest acts of sacrifice or courage or love. Our intuitions differ a bit as to which particular cases we find most compelling, and they differ more across time and culture. But there are strong resemblances across individuals, times, and cultures. We are insistently moralistic creatures, with strong moral emotions and impulses, especially around issues like fairness, cheating, betrayal, cruelty, and suffering.[44] We constantly judge and praise and blame, and we insist that some things are really, truly right while others are really, truly wrong. This comports very well with the moral realism that can be justified by a variety of religious views.

Many of us also have strong intuitions that life has meaning, although these aren't as universal as our moral intuitions. Certainly many people feel that all human life is valuable or meaningful, and this is often expressed in language of human dignity or human rights. But such feelings are not universal, and the brutality of history suggests that they used to be rarer. And as we narrow the circle of concern from all humans to one's country, race, tribe, or family, it becomes less clear that there's any notion of life's value or meaning at work. Someone can defend the members of his family simply because he likes them or needs them, without having any inkling of life being valuable or meaningful in itself. But inasmuch as there is pressure to justify intuitions that life has meaning, this too fits very well with religious accounts that see life as truly meaningful.

This match between intuition and religion is what we might expect. This holds whether God created us with purpose and value and moral duties, or instead we are part of an impersonal moral and spiritual order, or instead no such thing is true and we've simply made up religions that suit us. But in that last case our intuitions do not have the sort of rational support they'd have on a religious picture of reality. To make this clear, we must first clarify what a nonreligious picture of reality is.

Today it's common to reject the full accounts of religions but then assert some vague notion of God or providence or an afterlife. Starting from scratch it certainly could be the case that all religions are false but still everything happens for a reason, or still everyone gets happiness or justice after death, or still there's someone out there to hear your prayers and give you signs on how to live. But what reason do we have to think that something like this is actually true? As discussed earlier, religious doctrines stand on their respective religious justifications, and the mere fact of commonalities between religious doctrines is not itself an alternative justification. We cannot sensibly reject all religious foundations but then still make lofty, if vague, religious claims, floating and unjustified. And sensible nonreligious views do not do this. They instead accept the material universe, of which we have such extensive sensory and scientific evidence, and then stop there, asserting nothing more. This is known as metaphysical naturalism, or simply naturalism.

Can naturalism rationally support the sorts of meaning and morality that are supported by religion and intuition? Certainly naturalism can acknowledge all the psychological and social phenomena we observe in the world, including the existence of our intuitions around meaning and morality, and the fact that most people, both religious and nonreligious, make moral claims, live moral lives,[45] and see life as meaningful. But these phenomena can be explained naturalistically, as resulting from our instincts and faculties as social animals, and as intelligent, linguistic, sense-making animals. It is a separate question whether the content of our intuitions is correct, and whether it can be rationally justified by naturalism in ways comparable to how it can be justified by religion. It could be the case that we've evolved minds that perceive real right and wrong and meaning in a world where such things are absent.

Some object that we would not evolve to believe false things, at least not on such a scale; or that if things we've evolved to believe are false but useful then that usefulness is enough to vindicate them. But these are misunderstandings. First, it's a simple matter that beliefs could be false but evolutionarily useful. One example is what's known as agent detection. It's better to detect prey where there is none and stab a bush than to make the opposite error and miss a meal. And it's better to detect a predator or enemy where there is none and flee than to make the opposite error and die. So our tendency toward false beliefs in the form of excessive agent detection is useful.[46] And there's no reason why this same dynamic could not arise with consistently false beliefs — as, perhaps, in the case of false moral beliefs that help us to coexist and cooperate. Meanwhile the usefulness of false beliefs may vindicate them in some senses, but it doesn't stop them from being false. And it's truth and falseness that are our present concern.

So it seems that naturalism can be used to explain intuitive and religious notions of meaning and morality without justifying them. But can it instead be used to justify them? Can naturalism rationally support the robust sorts of meaning and morality that are supported by religion?

Attempts are certainly made. Sophisticated accounts are given of what's special about human life, or how notions like human rights contribute to a happier world, or how a moral code can be derived from seeing all people as equal, or how a moral code can maximize pleasure and minimize pain. But these things are beside the point. They do not address the questions we're currently asking. Concerning notions of the value or meaning of human life, we're asking not whether they work but whether they're true. And this truth is not established merely by pointing to aspects of life we like or pointing to distinguishing features of our species, comparable to the other distinguishing features of other species. As for morality, the accounts mentioned above focus, like the great bulk of moral philosophy, on substantive ethics rather than meta-ethics, arguing about what distinguishes rightness from wrongness and which actions fall under each heading without ever adequately establishing what the two headings actually are.[47] But that's the question we're now asking. On religious accounts right and wrong are woven into the fabric of reality, just as real and fundamental as the laws of physics. No such thing is true under naturalism.

The reality is that supernatural claims support supernatural accounts of meaning and morality, and supernatural meaning and morality match our intuitions, whether because some supernatural reality determined us or because all supernatural stories were determined by us. And supernatural meaning and morality simply cannot be supported by a naturalistic picture of reality. This should not be surprising. In fact it would be surprising if it were otherwise.

Some reply that life is just as meaningful without religion, or is even more meaningful; and that naturalists can be good without God, or even that naturalism is more conducive to goodness. But this too is beside the point. We are currently asking what follows rationally from religion and from naturalism. What people think and feel and do is another matter.

In light of all this we face a dilemma, and a sort of argument for religion. Our intuitions around meaning and morality can be supported by religion in ways that they cannot be supported without it. So either we embrace some religious account that justifies our intuitions, or else we see our intuitions as unjustified. We can put the intuitions on a religious footing, or we can give them up.

\* \* \*

Another type of argument for religion starts with our human longings for spiritual realities like God or eternal life, and sees those longings as evidence of the things longed for, claiming that the longings would not exist if their objects did not exist. Granted, spiritual longings are phenomena that need to be explained, so it's right to consider them. But it's wrong to draw from them such hasty and convenient conclusions. The question is how we can best explain the varied phenomena of spiritual longing.[48] And one possible explanation is indeed that the objects of our spiritual longings exist. It's possible, for example, that our longing for God points us to a God who designed us to long for him, or that we long for eternal life because we are immortal souls living life after life in body after body.

But are there alternative explanations? And are there any alternatives that explain the phenomena just as well without introducing huge metaphysical claims?

It turns out that there are. With spiritual longings, as with intuitions around meaning and morality, the phenomena in question can be explained by naturalism alone. A naturalistic picture of our evolution into intelligent social animals with language is sufficient to explain how we might end up longing for supernatural things. In broad strokes,[49] it seems that a longing for eternal life, for example, could arise from the combination of naturalistic elements like our animal drive for self-preservation, our disconcerting knowledge that we'll die, our social bonds with the living, and our ability to imagine and describe scenarios in which death is not the end. And it seems that a longing for God could arise from naturalistic elements like our formative attachment to and dependence on parents, our comfort with hierarchy and authority, our curiosity about the world, and our comfort with the sorts of intentional and teleological explanations that a God could support. In both examples the central idea is that a naturalistic universe could have created, through evolution, beings who in some sense want or expect the supernatural. This is an idea to which we'll return.

\* \* \*

Other arguments urge a bet or choice in favor of religion under conditions of uncertainty. The goal of these arguments is not to make us confident that religious claims are true but to give us reason to embrace such claims even without such confidence. One sort of argument stresses the infinite rewards and punishments described by many religions and argues that they make it prudent to bet on religion. If you bet on such a religion and win, then your winnings are infinite, while if you bet against such a religion and lose, your losses are infinite. This contrasts with the comparably meager gain of getting to ignore religion, or the comparably meager loss of betting on religion but winning nothing. So, the argument goes, bet on religion.

Another sort of argument claims that religious faith is meant to be not a mechanical conclusion but partly or wholly a volitional choice, perhaps even a difficult one. So God, or the spiritual order, has placed us in an uncertain situation by design, and we're meant to choose religion in the absence of conclusive evidence, or even in the face of contrary evidence. These arguments sometimes draw on features of a particular religious tradition stressing faith, hope, trust, or commitment.

Some object that the betting or choosing counseled by such arguments is insincere, mercenary, or otherwise inadequate. Put in terms of belief, some say religious belief that's chosen in such a way would not be genuine, or that it is difficult or impossible to determine beliefs by a raw act of will. One response is to frame the choice to believe not as a matter of a single instant but rather as a choice to cultivate belief over time through actions like associating with believers, praying or meditating, reading scripture and apologetics, and living morally.

Another objection, though, concerns the issue of which particular religious beliefs one is supposed to bet on, choose, or cultivate. In framing the bet above, there were two possibilities: betting on religion and betting against it. And this framing may feel appropriate in cultural contexts with one overwhelmingly dominant religion. But there are in fact hundreds of religions in the world, and thousands throughout history, and infinite possible religions. If we want to bet on religion, what can lead us toward one rather than all the others?[50] That's where we'll now turn.

\* \* \*

We've seen that religious claims are epistemically based on the special spiritual knowledge claimed by the religion's sacred texts, teachers, or institutions. This is where the most promising arguments for particular religions focus, trying to establish that a text came from God, a teacher heard from God, an institution was founded and guided by God, etc. The most common way to support such claims is through miracles, so that's where we'll begin.

A miracle would be roughly something that cannot be explained naturalistically and is instead explained by the supernatural realities described by a religion. If the occurrence of such a miracle could be established, this would show that the supernatural realities in question do in fact exist, and might also show that the religion in question has some privileged connection with those realities.

Some people reject miracles as a contradiction in terms, arguing that an event would only qualify as a miracle if it broke the laws of nature, but those laws are unbreakable. But this begs the question, and merely shows that when we define something as impossible, it is, on that definition, impossible. But it's hard to see anything impossible or even difficult in the idea of, for example, a God who created and sustains the entire universe, including the laws that govern its normal operation, then choosing to reach in and make particular adjustments.

But while I see no conceptual problem with miracles, practical problems abound. It seems that we're inclined to accept many miraculous claims that have little rational justification. We're quick, for example, to perceive a miracle when someone survives a terrible accident or recovers from a terrible illness. But before taking any such event as evidence for a religious claim we need to distinguish between an event that *might* be a miracle, on the one hand, and one that *must* be a miracle, on the other. For if we assume the existence of a God or some other potential source of miracles, then countless events in the world become potential miracles, and I'm making no attempt here to judge most of these events. I'm concerned only with the narrow subset of events[51] that *must* be miracles, in the sense that they *absolutely cannot* be explained naturalistically,[52] and therefore count as evidence for the existence of something supernatural.

In contrast when something occurs that's just very unlikely, well, it's likely to occur plenty of times in a world of nearly 8 billion people. Someone surviving an illness with a 1% survival rate is not supernatural but is the expected complement to 99 people who die of that illness. And someone walking away from a mangled car wreck is not supernatural but is the complement of all those who die in similarly mangled wrecks.[53]

But what about more emphatic miracles? What about raising the dead, parting the sea, or ascending into the sky?

First, it's a problem if one merely hears about such miracles instead of witnessing them. Because no matter how earnestly and sincerely someone tells you about a particular miracle that supports his particular religion, for you this will stand alongside equally earnest and sincere reports of other miracles that support contradictory religions.[54] And this holds whether you're hearing the reports in person or reading them in sacred texts.

The situation is different if there's any reader who has directly perceived something that is not merely unlikely but is naturalistically impossible. But even then, difficulties remain. For we sometimes perceive things that are not really there. In conditions of stress, exhaustion, hunger, or intoxication we sometimes perceive what's not actually occurring. And the supernatural occurrences perceived in such states have a remarkable tendency to match our cultural expectations, so that, for example, lying on one's deathbed or after an extended fast, an animist sees spirits while a Hindu sees Krishna while a Christian sees Christ. The vividness and intensity of such experiences often leave a person with unshakeable certainty. But rationally speaking there seems to be reason for doubt.

Another sort of miracle would be to know something by supernatural means that couldn't be known by any natural means. If someone ascended high enough in holiness or wisdom to see realities to which others were blind, or if a God chose to tell us things we couldn't have otherwise learned, this could provide evidence for religious claims.

To serve this evidentiary function, though, it must be a definite statement of something that we now know to be true but that, at the time it was first stated, we could not have known by any natural means. For if it was at the time knowable through natural means then it needs no special explanation, and likewise if it was unknowable at the time and remains unknowable today.

It seems that what would be needed, then, is either predictive prophecies that we know were later fulfilled, or statements of truths that weren't known at the time but have since been confirmed by explorers or scientists. But it would need to be clear that we were dealing with knowledge that naturalism cannot explain, and not merely guesswork or mystification that naturalism can quite easily explain. More precisely it would need to be clear that the supposed knowledge was not just a lucky guess; is not having its meaning projected only in hindsight onto words that are in themselves vague, cryptic, metaphorical, or concerned with something unrelated; was not just one prediction among many, with some sort of selective interpretation used to see the one as true without seeing the many as false; was not a later forgery that was actually produced after the knowledge was known naturalistically; and did not motivate people to do the very thing it predicted would be done.

Those are just five simple and sensible requirements. Any supernatural intelligence choosing to reveal itself could easily satisfy them,[55] and would see the need to do so if it wanted its revelation to be distinguishable from all the competing messages produced through merely human means.[56] But of all the world's proud claims to spiritual insight or divine revelation, there's not even one that meets these five requirements.[57]

* * *

There are several remaining types of arguments for particular religions or general religious claims that should be addressed but can be addressed briefly. We'll then turn our attention to positive arguments against religious claims,[58] and then finally step back and take stock.

Many religious individuals embrace their religion and commend it to others on the basis of things like answered prayer, miracles reported in sacred texts, positive effects on one's life, and emotional experiences in prayer, meditation, or worship. The first point to notice is that the same reasons are used to support contradictory religions, and therefore cannot help us choose among religions. And we've already seen further problems with miracles, and especially second-hand reports of miracles. As for the emotional resonance of prayer, meditation, and worship, we would expect such resonance whether religion tells the truth about supernatural reality and how we're meant to relate to it or is instead only what we've created and modified and transmitted in ways we've found resonant. The same goes for practical and psychological benefits of religion.

Answered prayer deserves some additional consideration. The first thing to note is our tendency to notice and remember things that support our beliefs while overlooking or forgetting things that don't. So a believer who prays for various outcomes will naturally tend to remember when those outcomes occur but forget when they don't. And similarly, someone who follows perceived divine guidance will tend to remember when this works out well and forget when it doesn't. In addition, with answered prayer, as with miracles and prophecies earlier, we need to distinguish between what can be seen as answered prayer if one already believes, and what clears a higher bar and gives us reason to begin believing in the first place. Generally claims of answered prayer fall squarely into the first category, and are no help to those who do not already believe.

Other religious arguments focus on the beauty of religious texts, liturgies, architecture, or artwork. But our perceptions of religious beauty are often conditioned by the very thing perceived as beautiful, through one's experiences with a religion early in life and through living in a culture influenced by the religion. Also these sorts arguments do nothing to help us distinguish among religions, because the aesthetic attraction of Muslims to the Quran, for example, seems matched by that of Hindus to the Vedas and that of Christians to the New Testament. And even if the Quran were somehow shown to be uniquely beautiful, it's not clear how this would support an inference to divine inspiration over an inference to simple literary achievement.

Other arguments see beauty or goodness in the effects of a religion as it contributes to desired outcomes for individuals or communities. This can focus on enduring religious civilizations, on stable local communities, on intense bonds between the most devout, on especially saintly individuals, or on particular virtues exemplified at any of these levels. But these arguments repeat the pattern by giving equal support to contradictory religions, and the effects they focus on seem to be easily explained by natural psychological and social forces.

Returning to more general religious claims, there are what are known as ontological arguments for the existence of God, claiming that God is the greatest being we can conceive of, having every conceivable sort of greatness, one of which is the greatness of actually existing. Some versions put this in terms of modal logic and claim that God is a necessary being, and if it's possible for this necessary being to exist then it necessarily exists. These arguments strike many people as mere word games that cannot demonstrate the existence of God in reality. And this is essentially correct. Because the operative question is whether it's possible that there's no God, and this question is best answered not by parsing definitions but by looking at reality, precisely as we've been doing.

Other arguments claim that our knowledge of God is a sort of direct apprehension, analogous to sensory perception. These arguments claim that just as we see the world and know it exists, without intervening arguments, we likewise perceive God and know he exists, without arguments. I don't dispute that those who believe can perceive God as pervasively and compellingly as we all perceive the world around us. But this sort of emphatic perception can apply equally to different Gods or even to the absence of God. It's simply a feature of human psychology that with time our opinions tend to seem increasingly correct and obvious to us, in matters of religion as elsewhere. And even if the perception of God were strong and universal, this alone still would not show that God actually exists.

Other arguments claim that investigations into religious matters should begin with a presumption of theism. We should start off believing God exists and only abandon this belief if it is refuted, which, it is argued, it never adequately is. This argument may have merit when it is opposed to a presumption of atheism.

But our investigation made use of neither presumption, and has instead worked to consider all competing claims on their own terms. It's difficult to argue that we should have instead begun by presuming the one very particular and robust conclusion of theism. And even if that were granted, the considerations in this chapter might be enough to rebut that presumption.

Lastly there are arguments that God is not something separate from the material universe, but rather the universe *is* God. These arguments end in one of two places. Either they bring in elements of intelligence and intention that we do not observe in the material universe, in which case they are making claims that need justification, which justification must be attempted along the lines of the arguments we've already covered; or else they refrain from doing this and simply express or urge attitudes like awe and gratitude toward the universe. There is much to commend such attitudes. But they do not amount to religious claims, and do not justify any distinctively religious conclusions or actions.

* * *

God is said to be all-powerful, all-knowing, and all-good. This is the conception of God that is explicitly or implicitly targeted by most positive arguments against the existence of God. Such arguments claim that these attributes conflict with one another, with other qualities or actions attributed to God, or with things we observe in the world. For example it is argued that if God is all-knowing then God knows all the actions he will take, and this renders him powerless to take all contrary actions, which means he's not all-powerful. Or it is claimed that our world, with all its suffering and injustice, is not what such a God would create.

Some responses claim that these challenges misconstrue the relevant divine attributes. So omnipotence, for example, does not mean that God can do whatever humans can say, some of which is actually nonsense, but rather it means than God has the power to take all logically possible actions. So God cannot create round squares, and God cannot create a rock too heavy for him to lift, not because he lacks the power to take these actions but because these are not really actions at all.

Other responses cut deeper by saying that God's power, knowledge, and goodness should be understood not as the abstractions of philosophers but as reflections of what is said of God in the right scriptures or traditions. And sometimes these scriptures and traditions stress their own limited and approximate nature, and stress the mystery and transcendence of God. Therefore, it is argued, a proper conception of God does not center on rigorous definitions of omnipotence and the rest, but on, for example, a scriptural revelation of a God who is wholly other and incomprehensible to his finite creatures, but has revealed himself to have all power and knowledge and goodness—without explaining precisely what this means. On the one hand this can seem like special pleading. But on the other hand, the idea that God could be beyond the comprehension of creatures he's made does seem sensible, and it was indeed central to many religious traditions long before any philosophers lodged their conceptual complaints.

Other arguments against the existence of God center on the suffering in the world. It is argued that a God who is all-good would want to create a world without suffering, a God who is all-knowing would know how to do so, and a God who is all-powerful could in fact do it. Therefore, since we observe suffering, no such God exists.

Some responses to these arguments carve off classes of suffering that contribute to good things like bravery or compassion, or that result from human freedom, which might be a good that's worth the cost. But there remains an incredible amount of human and animal suffering from sources like illness, parasites, predation, and natural disasters that brings no discernible benefit to the sufferer or anyone else. Can such suffering be reconciled with the existence of a good God?

The answer seems to depend on what our notion of goodness is. If God is a utilitarian who wants to maximize pleasure and minimize pain, then it seems that our world is not the world he would create. Or put another way, it seems that we can conclude from our world that no utilitarian God exists.

But it could be that God exists and simply has other goals in mind. It could be that God is indeed focused on human well-being, but this well-being in fact has little to do with pleasure during this life and much more to do with things like moral development, faith, struggle, endurance, and even suffering itself. Or it could be that God is less focused on human well-being than on his own pleasure and glory, and these are better served by this world than by its softer alternatives. Ideas along these lines occur in many religious traditions. And of course, many traditions claim that earthly sufferings will be far outweighed by heavenly bliss.

\* \* \*

Earlier we examined arguments for the existence of God that drew on biological realities. But other arguments claim that biological realities actually disprove the existence of God. It's argued that evolution's slow and indirect progress, full of suffering and death and extinction, is not how a God would choose to create; or that the structural products of evolution that we observe, which are often stunning and elegant, but at other times rickety and suboptimal, are not what a God would create. The problem with such arguments is that they assume a great deal about the will of the God they reject. It's certainly valid to note that both living organisms and the archaeological record display messy evolution rather than neat and direct creation. But it's harder to establish that a God would take the latter path instead of the former. Particular religions that assert this do indeed face problems with the messiness of evolution. But this messiness does not refute the general possibility of a God.

Things are much the same for the size and age of the universe, and the rarity of life within it. Some argue that our universe of vast barren expanses, filled with violent forces that prevent or destroy life in nearly all places, where almost 10 billion years passed before the first simple life arose on earth and over 99.99% of history passed before anatomically modern humans arose — this is not the work of a God creating life. And such arguments do indeed pose problems for religions that assert or imply contrary facts. But here, as with evolution, they do nothing to refute the general possibility of a God.

Other arguments assert that the inconsistent revelations claimed by different religions prove that there is no God, or at least create a situation in which it's difficult or unreasonable to believe in God. Some claim that a God would not allow our present situation in which inconsistent divine revelations are commended to us on the same grounds, or that the God of the one true religion would not allow so many contrary religions to have comparable support. These arguments underscore the difficulty of choosing among religions, which we've already noted. But they do nothing to undermine possibilities like a God who is equally happy with adherence to any religion, or a God who is indifferent to human religious belief and practice.

Other arguments against the existence of God focus on particular things that religions attribute to God. For example, it is argued that God would not alter his plans or intervene in his lawlike universe in order to answer prayers, or that God would not condemn anyone to eternal suffering in hell. But these are properly understood as arguments against the doctrines in question or the religions that teach them, and not against the existence of God, since these arguments do nothing to disprove the existence of a God not described by such doctrines.

\* \* \*

We can now step back and survey the whole logical landscape. We've seen no single argument that proves the existence of God, of souls, or of any other supernatural reality. And we've seen no arguments that can distinguish any one religion from the rest. But we have seen arguments that give real support to religious views. We've seen that scientists understand a tremendous amount about how the universe came about and how life came about within it, and that this understanding involves natural processes that do not require any supernatural explanation. But it also involves parameters perfect to allow life in ways that their alternatives would not, and it involves gaps concerning how life first arose and concerning the Big Bang's cause or lack thereof. We've also seen that our intuitions around meaning and morality can be supported by religion in ways that they cannot be supported without it. If we are children of God or parts of some cosmic moral order, then this can rationally support belief in things like deep metaphysical meaning, robust moral obligations, and justice after death. But nothing comparable is supported if we're purely products of a naturalistic universe.

Taken together, these considerations create a rational pressure toward religious belief, which then leads us to prospects of choosing or betting on religion, and to questions of how to pick among competing religions. And they do indeed compete, so we must indeed pick. Although different religions have much in common, and secular thought often downplays their differences, those differences are very real, and are taken very seriously by religions themselves. On both abstract and practical matters there are many divergences and outright contradictions. For example many religions have multiple Gods, while the Abrahamic religions insist that there is only one God and that the point is crucial. Most Christians see this God as a Trinity of Father, Son, and Holy Spirit, while Muslims revere Jesus as a prophet but insist that God is unitary and has no son. And in daily life religions make incompatible demands on issues as tangible as money, food, sex, and marriage.

As we've already seen, no particular religion is able to distinguish itself from the rest on grounds like miracles, prophecies, saintly adherents, healthy communities, or beautiful worship. Instead each religion is commended to us on the same grounds as countless other religions.

In this context, notions of choosing religion or betting on religion get no traction. Such approaches might work if we faced a binary choice between belief and unbelief, but we do not, so they collapse.

Where does this leave us? We are unable to prove anything with certainty. But we are still forced to choose, simply in virtue of living. We will inevitably think and act in some ways and not others, which will inevitably comport with some accounts of reality and not others. Certainly it is possible to muddle along without reflecting or consciously choosing, and certainly this path is a well-traveled one. But it is not the path of this book. So let's consider what we might, upon reflection, consciously choose.

We are uncertain whether any supernatural reality exists. If we choose to believe and live as if none exists then this leaves us with gaps in our understandings of fundamental physics, a possible cause of the Big Bang, and how exactly the first life arose. Science has a long history of closing such gaps, so sooner or later these too may close. But it would not be especially surprising or worrisome if they did not. Because these are questions of the greatest abstraction and the most distant past, and we have no good reason to expect to learn their answers. People sometimes talk as if science should be able to answer all questions, but this is a deep misunderstanding. Science is not a divine revelation of all truth; it is a human effort to observe and decipher what we can. It's not surprising that some things may lie beyond the reach of science, during our lifetimes or even for all time. What's surprising is how far science has already reached.

The much bigger challenges for naturalism concern meaning and morality. Here the reflective and consistent naturalist must abandon many deep intuitions and hopes. The potent sorts of realism justified by supernaturalism must be abandoned. It must be admitted that while humans care about human life and values and morality, nothing in the wider universe does. We're obligated to no cosmic law or lawgiver, and we're never held to account. The only justice, the only reward for goodness, the only punishment for evil,[59] the only help for victims, is what we ourselves bring about in this life.

We can instead choose supernaturalism, but the choice now looks like a difficult one. We can postulate something to ground our meaning and morality and to fill the present gaps in our scientific knowledge, but doing so now looks like naked wish-fulfillment.[60] We can posit something that tidily answers our deepest questions, but then how deeply can we really believe those answers? Religion may be a way of giving ourselves such answers and obscuring the fact that that's what we've done. And it may work well enough while it remains obscure. But once we see clearly, it's hard to unsee.

If we manage this leap to supernaturalism, though, we can either leave off at some sort of Deism that answers whatever questions we find most pressing and goes no further, or we can make another leap to some fuller religion. We've seen that no religion distinguishes itself on rational grounds, so we can leap to the religion we'd prefer or to the religion we find most beautiful or resonant, which is likely to be the religion of our upbringing or our cultural surroundings. In any of these cases, though, the choice will be difficult to justify to ourselves or hide from ourselves.

And many particular religions erect a further barrier. For many religions laud ideals of truth and honesty, and present themselves not merely as useful or inspiring stories but as revelations of truth, filled with claims of historical, scientific, and metaphysical fact. So to the extent that naturalism appears likely to be true, these religions bar the way in.

Therefore, inasmuch as we want to believe true things, or want to be rational, or cannot bring ourselves to override our rationality, it seems we must make our peace with naturalism.

---

26. Some thinkers oppose what they call foundationalism, claiming that it requires a bedrock of certainty that's not possible. For related reasons some oppose the correspondence theory of truth discussed in chapter 1 and instead advocate judgments based on coherence, usefulness, or stability after prolonged inquiry. Such views are partially correct, since certainty is indeed impossible, and we are indeed forced to reason in provisional and iterative ways that draw on things like coherence, usefulness, and stability. But ultimately our paradigm, and therefore our descriptions and metaphors, should center on correspondence and foundations, because our present inquiry is less concerned with whether beliefs cohere, persist, or prove useful than with whether they match reality, stacking one truth upon another as they match one piece of reality after another, with sound arguments supporting true conclusions that in turn support other sound arguments to other true conclusions. So it's essential to examine chains of justification running all the way down to our most foundational justifications. Those foundational justifications won't be certain, but they are nonetheless the foundations on which everything rests.

27. Not that this is likely to result in people actually agreeing on religious matters. Even when conclusions are logically inescapable, psychological escapes always remain. Our minds and our languages are simply too agile for us to ever be led to any conclusion against

our will. But for any reader whose will is to eschew easy evasions in favor of hard truths, this book will show the way.

28. Here is a more precise description of the epistemic agreement I'm referencing. Across all varieties of religious and nonreligious thought, few people are willing to squarely repudiate reason or evidence. And those who attempt to do so—or to otherwise reject the central conclusions of chapters 1 and 2 that leave us reasoning about reality, bound by laws of non-contradiction and the excluded middle, and attending to reliable evidence about reality—cannot answer the challenges I've presented. In addition, on an experiential level it seems that we all tend to see ourselves as reasonable and our beliefs as supported by suitable evidence, and when challenged we immediately start reasoning in our defense and citing putative evidence.

29. To clarify some finer points, this section uses both the framing of true belief and the framing of action. The two are sometimes closely connected, as in cases like holding a true belief about a harmful action, but they can also diverge in various ways. And the two frames give rise to different divisions of the envisioned circle of screamed claims and demands. Within the framing of true belief, we're hoping to move toward the one set of claims that is entirely true (or, toward the one set of claims that is the truest set, or is the truest set regarding the most important beliefs, etc.), and to help us do this we're looking for whatever sorts of justification support true claims more strongly than they support any false claims. Our situation within the framing of action could be basically the same, but only if true beliefs matter in issues of religion. One case of this would be if there is in fact a God who wants you to believe true things about him. But even there, religious believers at different places along the circle disagree about whether God requires you to believe the precise truths of the truest sect, or only the broad truths of the right religion, or only the even broader truths common across religions. If the reality is instead that there's no God or other spiritual reality that cares what you believe, then it could be argued that all demands made of you

around the circle are equally wrong and you're utterly free. Or it could be argued that the standard for action becomes whatever makes you happy, or whatever contributes to the most happiness throughout society, or something along those lines. But note that any such judgments lie downstream from judgments about what's true in religious matters. So the framing of true belief is the one that will take precedence.

30. It is sometimes argued that certain forms of religion do not involve this paradigm, and instead limit themselves to a paradigm along the lines of "try this, it will work," with relevant teachers having only the status of inventors or explorers, rather than any status as seers or prophets or mediums. But such a paradigm is too limited to produce anything recognizable as religion. It can produce recommendations like meditating to feel more peaceful, if you already have a goal of feeling more peaceful. But it cannot tell you to meditate on the cycle of rebirth you're caught in, or on God's love for you, because that would introduce massive truth claims that lie far from "try this, it will work"; and it cannot tell you what goals to pursue.

31. Other claims are made in religious contexts but are not epistemically dependent upon a religion's foundational texts, teachers, or institutions. For example, when it's said by religious teachers or sacred texts that friendship is pleasant or that everybody dies, this needs no special religious justification. But such claims are not generally points of religious disagreement, and are not our present concern.

32. Meaning wrong in some definite and particular sense, to be held constant throughout this discussion.

33. Those grounds could include the fact of religious agreement, but more would need to be said.

34. Plus here it's not even clear that the inconsistent arguments actually converge in their conclusions. Some of the respective practices built on the respective conclusions can be characterized in the same terms, e.g. as "spirituality," but it is not as if each religion supports a generic claim that spirituality is good in the same way they do, at

least arguably, support the general claim that murder is bad.

35. It is variously referred to as evolution, evolution by natural selection, evolution by natural and sexual selection (to flag the powerful forces of sexual selection that operate in addition to the selective forces outside of a species), Darwinian evolution, and neo-Darwinian evolution (to flag the ways that evolutionary theory has developed in light of the knowledge of genetics that's been gained since Darwin's time).

36. Constructions like this about religions telling stories or making claims or taking actions are of course shorthand. Religions are comprised of thoughts and actions of individuals, and such shorthand points to such individual thoughts and actions, especially as aggregated in relevant communities or institutions, and reflected in the statements they embrace.

37. This point also addresses arguments that posit some fundamental difference between life and nonlife, and argue that living things could not arise from nonliving matter. The simplest self-replicating crystals or molecules may or may not be sensibly described as living, but they would seem to be a plausible bridge between whatever we mean by those two categories, being on the one hand just matter following physical laws, and on the other hand part of a process of causation and descent that leads gradually and continuously toward forms of life that we'd readily recognize as such.

38. This sort of reference to the brain is a bit of a shorthand, since the rest of the body keeps the brain alive and sends it all manner of electrical and chemical signals. But for simplicity I'll just refer to the brain.

39. Or spirit. Or atman. Note that if you're an adherent of a religious sect that's touchy about terminology or about finer points of doctrine, you'll need to do some translating in order to engage with what I write. Or of course you can refuse to do so, but that's one of the stupider ways to avoid engaging.

40. The sketch that follows above reflects points of agreement among most Jews, Christians, and Muslims throughout history, which

agreement is sometimes referred to as traditional theism or classical theism, and is shared by many adherents of other religions.

41. The problem, as we will see, is that this tremendous explanatory power of religion works equally well for countless contradictory religions. Also, to clarify, by "rooting everything in the material universe" I mean seeing everything as rooted in the material universe, or explaining everything by reference to only the material universe. If that grammar seems problematic because what's being explained by reference to the universe is itself part of the universe, a rephrasing would be something like "explaining all phenomena by reference to only the material universe," where one begins with a phenomenon that needs explaining and may or may not be entirely part of the material universe, and one ends up concluding that the phenomenon is in fact entirely part of the material universe.

42. Going further, this picture can grant that God's will might have been different, in moral matters and elsewhere, or it can instead claim that God's will is an expression of his unchanging nature or character, such that it could not actually have been different. And it can entertain questions about God's reasons for willing and creating as he did — including in terms of God's nature or character, or in terms of logical possibility and necessity — or it can instead claim that such questions are actually incoherent, because God faces none of the external forces or constraints that give rise to reasons on the human level.

43. Some handlings of the Euthyphro dilemma center on this idea.

44. And for many authority, respect, sanctity, and purity.

45. Here and elsewhere, I intend the claim that people act or live morally to mean that people act or live in what they perceive to be a moral manner. I do not intend such statements to imply the actual existence or nonexistence of a moral standard, or actual conformity or nonconformity to such a standard. When I intend to speak to such issues I'll do so explicitly.

46. This could be especially relevant to religion. Our excessive tendency to see agents could lead us to see spirits and Gods where there are none.

47. One common fallacy here is to hold some sense of rightness and wrongness constant and go hunting for referents; to assume that rightness and wrongness are real and important and then search for something, anything, to ground them in. But if we never expose rightness and wrongness to the risk of being negated then we can never really assert them either.

48. I will not presently attempt to characterize such longings or take any position on whether they are in various senses universal. For our purposes we can grant any account that a religious apologist might want to offer.

49. Broad strokes are appropriate here, for this is a matter of potentially removing support for religion, namely the type of support that says supernatural explanations are needed because natural ones are inadequate. Therefore all we need is a rough idea of how naturalistic evolution could have caused the phenomena of spiritual longing, and not a precise explanation of how it actually did.

50. As noted earlier, this question is indeed necessary. Starting from scratch it certainly could be the case that all religions are good and we need merely to embrace one, any one. But we've seen no adequate reason to think this is actually the case.

51. Perhaps so narrow that it's an empty set.

52. The question is whether a purported miracle can possibly be explained by some naturalistic picture of reality that's consistent with our present scientific knowledge. Note that the question is *not* whether a purported miracle can be fully and precisely explained by that present scientific knowledge itself.

53. In addition, cars are painstakingly engineered to absorb as much energy as possible in a crash while keeping the passenger compartment relatively intact, so often passengers are able to walk away precisely because the wreck looks so mangled.

54. By contradictory religions I mean religions that make contradictory claims, or, more operationally, religious communities or institutions that make contradictory claims. Some such contradictions might deserve to be forgiven, such as contradictions between two sets

of metaphorical language that could plausibly refer to the same underlying facts. But other contradictions are more central, explicit, and stubborn, such as that between the Christian dogma that Jesus is the Son of God and the Muslim dogma that God has no son, with their joint insistence that the point is essential; or the contradiction between the Jain imperative to do no harm and the jihadist imperative to harm infidels.

55. For example, "I have made you from tiny parts you cannot see, which work wondrously and have many parts of their own. Likewise have I made all living things." Or, "I have made water from three parts, two that are alike and one that is different. The two that are alike have a center of one, while the one that is different has a center of eight."

56. In the alternative paradigm of wise or holy individuals attaining special knowledge of spiritual realities we might have less reason to expect such things, but the epistemic need for them remains.

57. Consider some examples that fail to meet these requirements. Any purported prophecy of a relatively common occurrence like war or famine could, unless augmented by clear and particular details, easily come true through dumb luck. Second, in hindsight it's easy to project historical or scientific truths onto the mystical, mythical, allegorical, and apocalyptic texts of religions, or to project them onto unrelated narratives. Examples include the many New Testament passages citing as prophecies fulfilled by Jesus various Old Testament passages that are on their face not thundering prophecies about a coming Messiah but rather historical narratives, or prophecies of near-term political or military events, or instructions for Jewish worship. Here, as with miracles more generally, it's important to distinguish between what *might* be a prophecy, on the one hand, and what *must* be a prophecy, on the other. It's certainly possible that a God who knew the future would choose to reveal it only in cryptic prophecies. So for those who already believe in such a God, countless texts become potential prophecies. But while we are investigating the very question of whether such a God exists such

potential prophecies do not in themselves give us any evidence. Third is the issue of using selective interpretation to sift through numerous prophecies—e.g. all those of Nostradamus, or of the prophet Isaiah, or of the entire Bible—find several that could be applied to events that occurred between the prophecies and the present, crown those few as fulfilled prophecies, and say that all the rest remain to be fulfilled in the future. (By now it should be coming into view that the five requirements I've formulated involve some overlap, and some particular faults could be explained equally well by different requirements. For example my second and third requirements both involve using the benefits of hindsight to credit a text with predicting what it did not in fact predict. And selective interpretation can enable a would-be prophet to make enough predictions that some will come true by dumb luck.) Fourth is the prospect of selling after-the-fact description as before-the-fact prediction. When Joseph Smith published the Book of Mormon in 1830, for example, no supernatural insight was required to describe the European discovery and conquest of North America. But when Mormons claim that this description was actually translated from golden plates made many centuries before Columbus, this recasts it as a divine prophecy. Last are prophecies that cause their own fulfillment, e.g. by motivating Jews to return to Israel or motivating Christians to spread Christianity around the world. Here again I am not saying this proves God wasn't involved. It's just that the facts can be explained without reference to God and therefore give us no evidence for God's existence.

58. Meaning, for example, arguments that God does not exist, as opposed to attacks on arguments that God does exist.

59. These uses of the terms "goodness" and "evil" are intended as shorthand for that which we typically regard as goodness or evil, without implying that such regarding is correct and such things truly are good or evil.

60. Not in a Freudian sense involving repression, but simply in the sense of believing what we wish were true.

# Chapter 4

# Thinking

Recall that we turned our attention to religion because of epistemic considerations, namely because various religious views might justify a general trust in our minds and a general expectation that the world will make sense to us. But we've now seen that such religious views are themselves unjustified. This leaves us without the simple confidence of seeing ourselves as souls progressing toward enlightenment or as divine creations built to find truth. Instead it seems that we are a messy result of what helped our ancestors to survive and reproduce in the environments where they evolved. And it seems that the universe is not the construction of a mind like ours, but is a matter of impersonal forces working over eons, with many aspects we might find hard to comprehend.

How deep does this cut? Does it merely mean that we should be circumspect about our inclinations, our biases, our weaknesses? Or does it have more radical consequences? Does it mean we cannot trust our minds at all? Does it mean that we cannot trust reason, or that we're incapable of being rational? Does this picture of reality undermine itself by casting doubt on the chain of reasoning that led us to this picture in the first place?

Chapter 1 established the rudiments of rationality, centered on the laws of non-contradiction and the excluded middle. We granted that these rudiments might be features of the human mind rather than features of the wider universe, and the naturalistic picture of the mind and the universe that we've now arrived at may make this more plausible. But the fact remains that even if the laws of logic are not features of the wider universe we are still essentially forced to see them that way if we want to continue thinking and speaking.

But even after we accept reason, does a naturalistic picture of our minds give us cause to doubt the conclusions we reason to, perhaps including the conclusion of naturalism? If we give up the naive confidence that might be justified by a supernatural picture, do we get swept all the way to radical skepticism?

The answer begins with the tangible successes of science. As discussed in chapter 2, scientific findings have given us extraordinary abilities to manipulate reality in ways that we couldn't dream of before we arrived at such findings. And this seems to show that our scientific practices, centered on methodical observation and careful reasoning, successfully teach us about reality. This offers strong vindication of science, of the careful rationality that is part of science, and of our minds when exercised under the discipline of science and rationality.

This helps us to draw the right conclusions from the fact that our minds are products of evolution. Some argue that evolution must have shaped our minds to produce true beliefs, but we've already seen that this isn't correct. Others argue the opposite, that evolution would shape minds with totally unreliable beliefs, but this isn't correct either. The truth is that evolution isn't focused on beliefs at all. Selective pressures act on behaviors rather than on beliefs or any other mental states. As organisms compete to survive and reproduce, what matters are actions like finding food, evading predators, and winning mates. Because mental states do not directly help or hurt survival or reproduction they are not directly selected, and in fact plenty of organisms seem to exist only on the level of reflexes, with no appreciable mental states. When mental states do arise, though, it is from, and in service of, behaviors that are already in place. So when organisms become sophisticated enough to appreciably *want* food or safety or mates, for example, the mental states of wanting may in one sense drive the behaviors, but in another sense the behaviors drive the mental states, because the mental states arise only inasmuch as they augment the behaviors that had long been in place.

Intense selective pressures will steer even the simplest organism's behavior toward approaching what's beneficial to it and avoiding what's harmful to it. Then over evolutionary time any lineages that develop mental states of attraction and aversion will face selective pressures to feel attraction toward what's beneficial and to feel aversion toward what's harmful. At whatever point any lineages develop mental states that can be analyzed in terms of true or false belief, it seems that they would tend toward truth, such as believing to be edible what is truly edible, or believing oneself to be in danger when one truly is in danger.[61] But as we've already seen, tendencies toward particular errors can easily arise when false positives and false negatives are unequally costly, and even consistent errors can arise if they tend to promote useful behavior.

In our own case, we've obviously evolved mental states in addition to behaviors. And we've evolved language, which is in part driven by mental states and in part drives them. For sometimes we have a particular mental state and then choose to express it in language, but at other times we enact some reflexive linguistic behavior, like justifying an action or negotiating for a resource or bonding with a potential mate or ally, and only in the act of speaking or afterward do we arrive at any corresponding conscious mental states.[62]

With linguistic behaviors as with mental states, selective pressures do not act directly on the content but rather on the tangible effects out in the world that bear on survival and reproduction. What matters evolutionarily is not whether you said or believed true things while justifying an action, negotiating for a resource, or bonding with a mate or ally. All that matters is whether it worked. And this is sometimes served by truth, sometimes by useful fictions, and sometimes by more pronounced deception of others and even of oneself.

As our linguistic behaviors and mental states move further from tangible matters of survival and reproduction they are likely to face less evolutionary pressure toward truth. And they can move very far indeed, given our intelligence, our capacity for abstraction, and the reach and flexibility of our languages. For example, if we feel aversion to something inedible, we're able not only to think that it's inedible, but also to think that it's poisonous, or it's rotten, or it's ritually unclean, or it's inhabited by evil spirits, or it's forbidden by God. Similarly, if we feel aversion to a person we're able to think that he is untrustworthy, or that he is hostile to us, or that he's secretly conspiring against us, or that he's using witchcraft against us. And while these examples are anchored in some concrete aversion that's relevant to survival and reproduction, we're also able to think about matters that are far removed from such concerns, like how the universe began or what happens after death.

When features of our minds lead to false beliefs about predators or poisonous foods, those false beliefs get us killed and so those features get selected against. But often when features of our minds lead to false beliefs about spirits or divine laws, either those false beliefs don't hurt us very quickly or directly, so those features aren't strongly selected against; or those features actually help us on the whole and are selected for. For example we are quick to detect patterns in the world, detect agents in the world, and seek ways to influence the world. And often this leads us to perform rituals and offer sacrifices to nonexistent gods, which is a real cost. But this cost is outweighed by the associated benefits for things like tool-making, hunting, agriculture, and science.

Another crucial factor here is our social nature. We have long been a social animal, existing in groups rather than in isolation, with an individual's survival and reproduction being determined by his ability to bond, cooperate, compete, and manipulate. This adds another layer between truth and evolutionary usefulness. Not only is it the case that selective pressures work on actions rather than on true words or thoughts, as already noted. In addition those actions are often selected not for any direct effect on the world but rather for the reactions they inspire in fellow human minds. And this opens the way for entire suites of belief and speech and action to evolve for their social usefulness, without reference to truth. The evolutionary test of your religious beliefs, for example, is not whether they truthfully describe the origin of the universe, the occupants of the heavens, or the coming afterlife; the test is how the things they lead you to say and do affect your survival and reproduction, primarily through how they are received by those around you.

We are now increasingly moving into what's known as evolutionary psychology, which gets criticized from different angles and with differing levels of merit. Most simply, some people reject evolutionary understandings of human psychology and behavior because they reject evolution. But we've already seen that scientists agree on the basis of overwhelming evidence that evolution is how life developed, including human life. And we've seen the problems with rejecting such evidence because you think it undermines conclusions you like or supports conclusions you dislike. Others oppose evolutionary psychology because of perceived moral or political implications. It's argued, for example, that things like infidelity, rape, and warfare are legitimized by acknowledging their evolutionary roots. But such arguments involve several confusions. First, here too it is illegitimate to reject evidence because we dislike its perceived implications. In addition, seeing an evolved tendency toward a behavior does not mean seeing that behavior as unavoidable, and certainly does not mean seeing that behavior as morally good. In fact studying evolutionary causes of our worst behaviors can be like studying the causes of a disease, with the hope of using what we learn in efforts at prevention and treatment.

The strongest criticisms of evolutionary psychology accuse it of being overly speculative, and merely imagining a series of just-so stories for how particular behaviors and traits could have evolved. Certainly this is a risk. It is possible to just dream up plausible accounts of how things might have evolved, including accounts that contradict one another. So we should indeed be wary of any account that involves more dreaming than evidence. But at the same time, if we approach evolutionary psychology in a circumspect way, and hold loosely to whatever is speculative, it can be very useful. Part of this usefulness lies in replacing whatever dreams we already have in mind with new dreams that might be correct, and that are at least the right sorts of dreams. Inasmuch as we are, due to our personal and cultural histories, used to seeing ourselves as divinely created souls or purely rational minds, for example, it can be very beneficial to instead move toward seeing ourselves as the evolved animals that we actually are, even when particular points of the evolutionary story are doubtful.

Other arguments around evolutionary psychology involve misunderstandings about evolution, and about how evolutionary explanations function. First, an explanation in terms of evolution does not exclude explanations in other terms. For example a psychological explanation in terms of evolution does not exclude explanations in terms of things like cultural forces or individual choices any more than an evolutionary explanation for a disease excludes explanations in terms of organs and cells. In both cases evolution explains everything, but it explains some things indirectly, through structures or forces which are themselves explained through evolution. Cultural forces and individual choices are perfectly at home in an evolutionary framework, as long as they too are seen ultimately as products of evolution.

Perhaps the greatest misunderstanding, though, is that of thinking that since evolution selects what is beneficial for survival and reproduction, everything that evolves must be beneficial for survival and reproduction. On its face this sounds sensible, even tautological, but it ignores the complexity of evolutionary processes. Evolution does indeed select what's beneficial for survival and reproduction, but it does so only by selecting among whatever alternatives find themselves competing in a given time and place, and only according to what aids survival and reproduction right then and there. And this means that what evolved over evolutionary time can be very different from what is currently optimal for survival and reproduction.

And the complex interactions among genes mean that often it's not a simple matter of which competing gene performs a single function best but of which functions best in the aggregate, within the entire genome and the entire organism it produces. This leaves plenty of room for a gene to be useful in the aggregate and therefore selected by evolution while still having some particular effects that are harmful.[63] And over evolutionary time, new things get built on top of old ones, which leaves a great deal of room for the persistence of things that were once selected because they were useful, but which have through changes in the organism or its environment now become harmful, but which are nonetheless so bound up with useful things that evolved later that in the aggregate the harmful thing is less harmful than its absence would be.

Lastly, in the case of our own evolution, it's crucial to appreciate that the environments in which we now live are radically different from those in which we did most of our evolving. This is a point where some evolutionary psychologists are criticized for assuming too much about the precise pace of evolution or the precise environments that most shaped us. But even on the most conservative assumptions, it's clear that we spent most of our history hunting and gathering in small groups rather than living in cities and staring at screens. In evolutionary terms, the global industrial economy that so deeply shapes our lives is brand new, and even writing and agriculture arose only a moment ago. So the environments we've now made are radically different from the environments that made us.

\* \* \*

Our minds evolved to help us survive and reproduce, and this is primarily a matter of useful action rather than true words or thoughts. But at the same time, we would expect a tendency toward truth, at least in the matters that bear most directly on survival and reproduction; and it seems that the careful reasoning and observation of science lead us to a great deal of truth. This suggests that our minds are neither perfect at finding truth nor hopeless at it, and should therefore be neither trusted nor dismissed, but critically examined in order to identify exactly where they are strong and where they are weak.

Scientists are doing precisely that, and some of their findings have already been mentioned. They've found that we systematically notice things that support our current beliefs and ignore things that undermine them. This makes it easy to maintain false beliefs, and to do so effortlessly and in good faith, seeing those beliefs confirmed everywhere while being blind to everywhere they're challenged. We are too quick to detect agents, actors, minds. This helps us survive by leaning toward the much less costly type of error in detecting prey, predators, and enemies, but it also distorts our view of reality by leading us to see spirits and gods and ghosts where they're absent, and to see focused human intention and conspiracy in what are actually impersonal social and economic forces. In general we are quick to detect patterns and causal connections. This helps us to detect them when they're present but also leads us to detect them when they're not, seeing patterns in randomness, signals in noise, causation in correlation.

In addition, the mind works much more by association than by inference. One thought follows another generally not because of a logical relationship between the two but because of historical or emotional associations in our minds. This lets us think quickly and efficiently, without the slow effort of conscious reasoning. But it also blinds us to very real logical relationships, leading us to miss valid inferences that don't jump out at us through any preexisting associations, and leading us to insist that a logical connection is present when we merely feel a strong association.

It's these sorts of associations, and the speed and ease with which they occur, that inspire most of our confidence in our beliefs. If asked to defend our confidence we may begin quite sincerely offering evidence and arguments, but they are only part of the story, and usually a small part. Typically we find the evidence and arguments only after the belief is already in place, and can confront opposing evidence and arguments that are just as strong as our own without flinching. Because beneath the surface words that are exchanged about evidence and arguments there is something much sturdier, and that's the feeling of confidence, of knowledge, of certainty, arising from our interlocking associations, from how coherent our thoughts seem, from how quickly and easily we think them.

One result of this reliance on association and coherence is that often we are more confident the less we know. The fewer data points the mind is working with the easier it is to produce a coherent and compelling story. Often an expert on a topic is attuned to all its difficulties while a novice is sure it's easy and obvious. Often those who know the least about the world think it's simple while those who know the most find it baffling.

Another aspect of coherence is that the mind works to build coherent pictures even from conflicting data. So when people are beautiful we tend to see them as more intelligent and kind than they really are, and when a law or policy has a downside that we find compelling then we tend to see it as bad across the board, with no upside at all. This yields simplified pictures of reality that are useful for decisive action but often wildly inaccurate.

Our drive for coherence also interacts with strong biases toward oneself and one's groups. We tend to overrate our own virtues, skills, and social standing. When we succeed at something we tend to credit it to our own goodness, but when we fail we blame outside factors.[64] And the weaknesses of memory help enable these things. We forget negative memories of ourselves and our groups, positively embellish what we do remember, do the opposite for individuals and groups we hate—and typically feel confident that what we remember is accurate and complete. Listen in on almost any interpersonal argument if you want to see these things in action. And the next time you're in such an argument, realize that your memory isn't as accurate as it feels, and you're probably not as blameless as you think.

\* \* \*

Most of our thinking occurs quickly and automatically. We experience confident intuitive judgments, and then generally our conscious mind cooperates, and steps in only to offer supporting rationalizations to others, or to ourselves, if the occasion arises. It's possible for the conscious mind to instead interrogate and overturn our automatic judgments, but this is exceedingly rare. Yet it's precisely what we must do if we want to move toward truth. Because our automatic judgments work well enough for navigating what's familiar and applying whatever we already believe, but they don't work nearly as well for scrutinizing what we believe or exploring what's unfamiliar. For that we must rely on conscious reasoning, and actively work against the ways that our automatic judgments would undermine or overrule it. It's like the way pilots learn to trust a plane's instruments over the visceral sense of movement and orientation from the body's own vestibular and proprioceptive systems. These systems work well on the ground, in conditions like those they evolved in, but can become disoriented in a speeding and swerving aircraft. In the same way our automatic judgments work well for navigating immediate physical and social conditions like those they evolved in, but not necessarily for answering big questions like those of philosophy, religion, or politics.

To use conscious reasoning to truly scrutinize our automatic judgments we must work to reason carefully and explicitly, constantly attending to rational justification. Normally we speak in loose and approximate ways, we trust our feelings of which ideas follow from which others, and we're satisfied with an idea's justification once it reaches some other idea we're confident in. But this leads only to rationalizations that are socially useful, and to applying and maintaining whatever we already believe. To truly scrutinize our beliefs, and have a chance at identifying and revising those that are false, we need to reason more formally and methodically.

This requires distinguishing sharply between valid logical inference and mere psychological association. If you think that one idea follows from another, you should be able to spell out precisely how it follows—meaning how it *must* follow, so that there's no possible way for the first idea to be true while the second is false. Trying to do this will often lead you to better understand what other ideas are also implicated, what assumptions you're making, what evidence you're relying on, and what uncertainties are involved. And it will sometimes lead you to realize that the second idea does not, in fact, follow like you'd thought it did.

As you reflect in this way, you'll naturally feel satisfied with the truth of some belief once its justification reaches down to some other belief that you confidently hold. But remember how easily we are deceived by coherence. Remember that merely fitting your beliefs together with one another is not enough, and countless people who disagree with you are able to fit their beliefs together just as tightly. Neither is it enough to trace a belief's justification down to another belief that's held by everyone around you, or that seems obviously true, or that's held by the preachers or politicians or intellectuals you trust. Those who disagree with you can produce these very same justifications. The only sort of justification we've found that reliably leads to truth, without giving equal support to competing falsehoods, is justification through reason and evidence—and this means using only this sort of justification, all the way down. Letting in even one belief that's not justified in this way can support countless false beliefs, no matter how carefully you reason afterward.

Thinking in this way is hard. It's hard to doubt what you know. It's hard to question thoughts that come so quickly and easily and feel so coherent. But one exercise that can help is to imagine that some long- and widely-held belief is instead a brand new claim. Imagine that you're not repeating a claim that you've believed your whole life or that is believed by your whole community, but you're instead making a completely novel claim, which no one else has ever made or defended or believed. Those who hear you make the claim will be shocked, and will ask you to explain what exactly you mean, and why exactly you think it's true. How will you answer?

As an example, consider the person who claims that there is an afterlife but does not embrace any particular religion. Many people find this claim plausible—but why? It's largely because of our social and historical context in which so many people have for so long believed in an afterlife for explicitly religious reasons. A claim of some generic afterlife gets taken seriously because it's familiar, and it coheres with many common beliefs and feelings. But imagine a context in which no one has ever thought of reincarnation or paradise or anything other than ceasing to exist at the moment of death. And someone then makes the brand new claim that death is not the end, and people continue on past death in some way. Everyone who heard this claim would be stunned. No one would have a clue what was meant by it or what reason there was to think it's true. The person making the claim would then be forced to attempt some genuine justification.

Reasoning in this way can be a very slow process. The words quickly volleyed back and forth in an argument are usually not this sort of reasoning but rather rationalization and rhetoric. It is the mind functioning quickly and automatically, directed primarily toward social goals rather than philosophical ones. We react to defend ourselves and our views, and out comes a stream of words that serve that end. It takes effort to override this reaction, slow the pace of thinking and speaking, and begin to genuinely reason. One way to aid this effort is to strain to listen charitably, and to spot and acknowledge the very best points made or implied by your opponent, while straining in the opposite direction for yourself, and pausing to consider whether the answers that come naturally to mind are really as good as they might sound or feel.

This can build into a more general effort to speak less and listen more. Or we can go further and not only listen to what is spoken but even seek out stronger arguments that others may have made, or that we may be able to construct ourselves. We can move away from futile arguments and toward constructive thought — and we can do this even when opponents aren't trying to do the same. This can involve wariness of the pleasure that we seem to take in speaking, in asserting, in knowing. We can drag ourselves away from the easy pleasures of believing and toward the hard work of learning.

---

61. Byzantine alternatives have been proposed, and are indeed possible, but there's no reason to think they would be common.

62. The word "conscious" can be used in different senses within this discussion. The sense I intend here is that which distinguishes between mental phenomena of which we are aware, like those experienced when weighing a choice, reading a book, or admiring a sunset, and mental phenomena of which we are unaware, like all the processing and synthesizing of impulses and sensory inputs that occur before becoming aware that you find someone attractive or that some place feels dangerous. I did not use the word "conscious" at earlier mentions of the mental states of nonhuman animals because in that context it is typically understood in a different sense, not to distinguish the mental phenomena we're aware of from those we aren't, but to distinguish our conscious mental phenomena, whether taken in that sense of awareness or in some other sense, from the mental phenomena of most or all nonhuman animals.

63. Or, more precisely, that are recognizably suboptimal, whether or not this amounts to more positive sorts of harm.

64. Interestingly, some of these tendencies seem to be absent or even inverted in those with depression. This could plausibly be seen either as an effect of depression or as a cause of it.

# Chapter 5

# Living

Our inquiry began with earnest practical questions about how to understand the world and live in it. We chased these questions across broad swaths of philosophy and related disciplines, and very gradually arrived at a particular picture of reality. This picture in some ways answers our questions, in some ways shows them to lack satisfying answers, and in some ways sets up further inquiry. It is a picture of a vast and ancient physical universe, and of our minds as the universe's recent[65] and accidental creations.[66] Our minds were shaped solely for aiding the survival and reproduction of the particular primates we are, in the particular environments where we evolved, but this shaping happened to give rise to[67] rich conscious experience, to constant perceptions and descriptions of reality, and to capacities for refining those descriptions through careful reasoning and observation.

The result is that in one sense we are at home in the universe, being fully a part of it and a product of it. But in another sense we are exiles, looking for a land we'll never find. For in many ways the sort of universe that we expect, that we are primed to perceive, that we would find both intellectually and emotionally satisfying—is simply not the universe that exists. In many ways the universe we were built *by* is not the universe we were built *for*.

This is because evolution built our minds to navigate the immediate physical and social realities upon which our survival depended, but when we turn from those immediate realities to broader questions like those of science or philosophy or religion, we come to the task with the wrong tools. But still we seek out such tasks, and start work without hesitation, confidently forming and defending opinion after opinion. We are simply too smart and curious, too verbal and social and normative, to be content with thinking and speaking only about matters of daily survival. Our nature draws us inexorably toward bigger questions—questions that we're ill-suited to answer.

Often it's the very same aspects of our nature that both help us to navigate what's most tangible and immediate but also keep us from understanding what's broader and more abstract. Our skill at detecting patterns helped us hunt and forage and farm, but it also leads us to see patterns of divine intervention or human conspiracy where in fact there are none. Our constant normativity helps us bond and cooperate and influence, but it also leads us to long for cosmic justice and meaning that do not exist. Our capacities for language and abstraction help us plan, coordinate, remember, teach, learn; but they also enable us to create and defend endless varieties of nonsense.

In these ways our minds clash with reality. In these ways we are built not for this alien universe we find ourselves in but for one that's more human, being in some ways smaller and simpler, and in other ways grander, loftier, suffused with meaning and intention and goodness. The matter is not as direct as having innate beliefs that are false, or having a direct instinct to pray to a God who doesn't exist. Rather it's a matter of examining the whole tangled outcome when all the complexities of our psychology collide with all the complexities of some description of reality.[68] It's a matter of how thoughts or statements can, at the end of all those myriad interactions, tend to strike us as plausible or comforting or beautiful, on the one hand, or to strike us as ridiculous or frightening or bleak, on the other. It's also a matter of the ways in which we're inclined to reject many truths and embrace many falsehoods. One mechanism involves precisely the pleasant and unpleasant feelings just noted, for we seek pleasure and flee pain, no less when they are psychological than when they are physical. Other mechanisms involve skewing our questions, perceptions, or inferences in ways that ultimately lead toward falsehoods.

In this state of exile, with these clashes between our minds and the broader realities they aim at, it can be a strange and difficult thing to reason toward true beliefs. We've examined this difficulty generally, and additional difficulties arise when trying to reason toward true beliefs about one's own life. The pace and complexity of daily life and inner life are simply not amenable to any exhaustive and precise understanding. And our many powerful feelings can easily overwhelm our fragile thinking. But here as elsewhere, rationality remains possible despite its difficulties.

It is possible to face life's torrent of events and emotions and ideas with careful reasoning. It is possible to use rational tools to bring order to the chaos by asking questions, drawing distinctions, enumerating factors, estimating probabilities.[69] Even when we're forced to guess about the future, or to choose among tragic options, or to navigate fierce internal conflicts, still it is possible to move from misery or panic or confusion toward peace; toward understanding as much as possible and then accepting the limits of that understanding; toward making intentional and settled choices, with settled acceptance of their costs and risks.[70]

Such prospects are the focus of this final chapter. We've found no path to the sorts of comprehensive codes for living that are offered by many systems of thought, so in the absence of any such code we will be working only at the level of how an individual might want to live, by her own lights. On that level, though, there's still much to commend rationality.

Some pursue rationality about their own lives in hopes of seeing clearly and acting with intentionality and control. Such things can be valued for their own sake, or as means to other ends like happiness or success.[71] We can also be drawn toward things like clarity, intentionality, and control by the ways that we reflexively see and present ourselves as already having them. Most of our thinking and feeling occurs automatically and non-rationally, but the curious fact is that we generally insist on seeing and presenting the results of these automatic processes as being intentional and reasonable. We have our desires, our preferences, our aversions, and in themselves they are never rational or irrational. But we generally insist on giving reasons, and thereby opting in to the reasoning game. While in principle we could simply let our feelings stand as brute facts of psychology, not requiring any rational justification, in practice we almost never do this. Instead we have our anxieties and fears, and then move to make predictions of harm. We feel negatively about a person, and then move to make claims about his character, his motivations, his future behaviors. We have our values, and then move to assert that their objects are not just things we value but are valuable in themselves. We have our desires, and then move to assert that they are normal, healthy, morally good; and move to predict that the objects of those desires will bring happiness and fulfillment. We have our preferences, and then move to explain why the objects of those preferences are better than the objects of contrary preferences.

We could simply stop at the feeling, but we almost never do. We incessantly offer reasons to justify ourselves and persuade others—probably because this is precisely what language evolved for.[72] But the content of such words and thoughts reaches out far beyond such social usefulness and makes definite claims about the wider world. These claims can be analyzed like any others, and can prove to be true or false like any others.

When the claims justifying a feeling turn out to be false this does not immediately disarm the feeling, of course. But in most cases we do have at least some degree of control. In most cases those who have the will and expend the effort can choose whether or not to immediately act on the feeling, and whether to strengthen or weaken the feeling over time.

But to ever reach that point of seeing a feeling as unjustified and trying to resist and weaken it, it is essential to clearly and consistently distinguish feelings from justifications. The feeling is whatever it is. And the mind automatically produces putative justifications for the feeling. If you try to reject such justifications, generally this has no direct effect upon the feeling, and does not stop the mind's automatic justifying. Instead the feeling remains as strong as ever, and the mind automatically produces new putative justifications, or defenses of the old ones. These too can be rationally examined, and can be rejected if they too are found wanting—but the feeling will still remain, and the mind will immediately produce still more justifications and defenses. This may never stop unless you choose to stop it. Our minds and our languages are so flexible that it's always possible to produce an argument that will hold at least some appeal. The only escape is through the discipline of slow and careful reasoning. Reason as formally and precisely as you can. Attend carefully to where there are sound inferences and where there are only looser associations. Force yourself to truly reason about the relevant feelings, rather than simply feeling in circles. Only in this way can an unjustified feeling be identified and resisted.

* * *

Many of our daily thoughts, feelings, and justifications draw on matters of meaning, morality, and religion that we examined earlier. We arrived at a conclusion of metaphysical naturalism, seeing no adequate reason to accept any of the supernatural claims that we meet in the world. But we were not absolutely certain of this conclusion. Does that fact counsel some sort of agnosticism? Should we go through life without asserting things like the existence of God or of an afterlife but still bearing those possibilities in mind? Should we live righteously just in case there turns out to be some sort of judgment after death? Should we pray occasionally just in case there turns out to be someone listening?

The answers to these questions depend upon one's priorities and one's judgments of the probabilities that particular supernatural claims are true. If one set of claims seemed likely enough to be true then it might be worth betting a whole life on, as discussed in chapter 3. But we saw that no religion distinguishes itself from the others through any rational justification. So whatever probability one might assign to a general religious claim, such as the existence of a Creator, gets split among the thousands of contradictory religions claiming to speak for the Creator, or among the infinite possible accounts of the Creator that we can construct, so that each account is left with only the tiniest sliver of possibility.

One can try to aggregate some of these slivers together by living in a way that might be pleasing to multiple possible Gods. But this encounters the problem that so many religions are emphatic about their particulars, and demand not just upstanding citizens who say generic prayers, for example, but devoted worshippers with particular beliefs, rituals, diets, and sex lives—often in contradiction of the particular demands of other religions. And the more that an attempt at generic religiosity looks like what was already favored by one's gut or one's culture, the less it looks like any real attempt to please a God.

And other priorities pull us in other directions. Those who prioritize thinking and living in a coherent way will be drawn to focus on the one story that seems to be true rather than on all the others that could, just conceivably, be true. Likewise for those who feel a moral or aesthetic attraction to ideals like truth and honesty. For such people it seems that the way forward is to truly embrace naturalism, and to think and live as if it is true, even while remaining open to learning otherwise.

To embrace naturalism requires thinking clearly about what it means for morality, for the meaning or significance of life, for the nature of the self, and for what happens to the self at death. As shown in chapter 3, there are commonalities among the notions of meaning and morality that are supported by our intuitions and our religions. They involve seeing meaning and morality as not only psychological phenomena but as woven into the fabric of reality beyond the psyche, as truths for us to learn and laws for us to follow. On such views there truly is a right way to live, and this rightness obligates us, and we'll one day face righteous consequences. On such views life is indeed important, and important to live rightly, and there is some grand structure of which we are a part and in which we are at home.

Naturalism supports nothing comparable. On a naturalistic picture our intuitions around meaning and morality result from our evolution as smart, social, linguistic animals. These intuitions probably help us to cooperate and bond, and to cope with the pains and uncertainties of life,[73] but they do not tell us true things about the world. We've echoed and augmented these intuitions with the religions we've created, and they too may be useful in many ways, but they too fail to tell us the truth about the world. The truth is that we have no external standard for behavior, there will be no cosmic reward for kindness or punishment for cruelty, our existence was not planned or intended, and the universe swirls on in utter indifference to us.

Many naturalists choose to speak about these matters in exceedingly diplomatic ways. They strategically redefine terms, artfully smuggle in connotations and associations, weave back and forth between speaking of subjective experience and objective reality, downplay the supernaturalism in various cultural and intuitive views, and end by saying things which sound palatable enough to those conditioned by intuition and religion, but which actually carry none of the palatable content.

For example, a religious person claims that kindness is good because God commands it. A naturalist then answers that yes, kindness is good, but it's good because our society values it rather than because of any divine commands. On the surface this sounds like substituting one justification or explanation for another, while holding constant the idea that kindness is good. But this is not at all what's happening. The religious person means that kindness is truly good, no matter how we feel about it; and we're obligated to be kind to one another, and will be judged accordingly. The naturalist merely points to the fact that his society values kindness. And what follows from this fact? Someone in that society who is unkind is certainly not, on the naturalist's view, dodging any cosmic obligation, or risking hell or a bad reincarnation. It's merely that he risks social disapproval, or perhaps legal sanction in some cases, if he happens to get caught. And even this holds only in those societies with such a view of kindness. Things would be inverted in a society that disdained kindness and valued brutality.

So is the naturalist offering the religious person a different explanation for the same moral goodness? Not at all. He's instead saying that the sort of goodness the religious person spoke of does not exist, nor does anything like it, but something that shares a few features is a social norm.

As another example, a religious person claims that the meaning of life is to come to know and love God, and a naturalist answers that no, the meaning of life is to pursue one's passions. The religious person means that God created humanity for the purpose of coming to know and love him, and doing so is the lofty obligation and privilege of every person, which can lead to blissful union with God in eternity. The naturalist means something along the lines that pursuing one's passions tends to give one pleasure or satisfaction. Pleasure and satisfaction are things we care about, so this is a notable claim—but it has little to do with the sort of meaning envisioned by the religious person. Where the religious person saw grand external intention, valuing, obligation, and reward, the naturalist sees nothing. So what the naturalist is really saying is that the sort of meaning the religious person spoke of does not exist, nor does anything like it, but something that shares a few features is pursuing one's passions.

More generally, if we set aside diplomacy and instead seek clarity, even bluntness, the truth is that according to the usual meanings of relevant terms, as intended by speakers and perceived by hearers, and as etched into the histories of our languages and cultures: nothing is right, nothing is wrong, and life has no meaning. Only once this stark reality is faced can we proceed with any honest discussion of how to live and value. Perhaps there are sorts of meaning and morality that can survive this realization, or can be rebuilt after it, but they cannot be clearly understood until this realization is faced. To honestly and consistently face naturalism requires giving up all supernaturalism, and everything that logically depends upon it. And in the case of meaning and morality, that's nearly everything.

* * *

A naturalistic picture of death is similarly unforgiving. There is no reason to expect any heaven, paradise, reincarnation, resurrection, or other persistence of your mind or self. You are not a soul that might go elsewhere when your body dies. Your mind is not some special unity or energy or essence that might continue without your body. You are a body, a brain, a complex organization of neurons and their chemical and electrical signals. From this arises some incredible abilities and experiences, including your experience of being a conscious self. But this experience arises wholly from the functioning of your brain, and it ends fully and finally when that functioning ends. When your brain ceases to function you cease to exist.

Plenty of people reject this account because they reject naturalism. But many others accept the naturalistic account in theory but then do a great deal to soften it in practice. Many simply suppress thoughts of death, while others think and speak loosely about how various effects of their lives might persist after their death, or how the people or institutions or ideas they care about will continue after their death, or even how the atoms and energy of their bodies will continue to exist—and from this they draw feelings that could be rationally justified by an afterlife but cannot be justified without one. To instead think clearly about death means to acknowledge its stark and absolute finality.

* * *

There is no ultimate right and wrong to guide our actions. But still we must act, and still our moral sensibilities are strong, and are largely similar from individual to individual. We are all the same social animal with the same moral instincts. These are not instincts that directly dictate specific actions, but rather suites of moral emotions like sympathy, gratitude, guilt, anger, and disgust, and bounded ranges of scenarios that can trigger each emotion. Large roles remain for factors like one's material surroundings, culture, upbringing, and beliefs, and these are the factors that cause moral judgments to converge within groups and to sometimes diverge between them.

And often tensions arise within individuals. We all think that others should treat us fairly, and many of us formulate universal rules about fairness, but when the right opportunity arises to take more than your fair share your mind may quickly supply reasons to see it as an exception. More generally, tensions arise between moral sensibilities and selfishness or opportunism; and inasmuch as moral sensibilities grant standing to outside groups, tensions also arise between moral sensibilities and group loyalty or chauvinism. This is exactly what we would expect from sensibilities that evolved to help an individual survive and reproduce, often by means of cooperation with other individuals, but always judged by the individual's own reproductive success.

In moral and political matters this creates substantial agreement as well as substantial challenges. But the agreement itself can provide a firm foundation to build from, relying only on the sensibilities that we do in fact share, across all or most individuals, or all or most individuals within a culture or a country, without needing to assert that various claims suggested by those sensibilities are actually true. Our aversion to murder, for example, can be adequate to personally and politically oppose murder without ever claiming that it is morally wrong.

Similarly, the desire for happiness[74] that we share may be enough to embrace it as a political goal, and is certainly enough to examine it here. The first thing to note is that we did not evolve to be happy. Happiness is evolution's tool rather than its goal. Happiness—especially brief happiness or expected happiness—is a lure to draw us toward behaviors that are useful for survival and reproduction. But if we desire happiness itself, especially as a relatively steady state, this may not always be served by our evolved impulses.

In some ways to seek a happy life is to seek to game the evolutionary system. It requires looking for ways that expected happiness can turn out to be brief, if not altogether illusory. And it requires looking for ways that feelings like discontentment, envy, anger, and resentment might goad us to acquire more resources but undermine our aggregate happiness. For anyone who prioritizes the goal of being happy over the goal of leaving as many offspring as possible, it will often make sense to refuse to act on such feelings, and to try to weaken them.

We can also attend to ways that our present environments

differ from those we evolved in. Our ancestors lived short and precarious lives in small groups on which they depended for survival. This has given us biases toward the present moment over the future we may never see that if left unchecked can create futures full of unnecessary tragedy, on personal, group, and global levels. It has also given us impulses to constantly evaluate one another, judging and confronting and gossiping in order to root out the lazy and disloyal who might bring death to the whole group, and in order to influence the group for our own personal advantage. But in the contemporary world these things often bring small and unnecessary material gains at huge emotional costs. So those seeking happiness can choose to resist and weaken these impulses.

Happiness also interacts in complex ways with beliefs around meaning, morality, death, and religion. Inasmuch as we are evolutionarily inclined or personally accustomed to false beliefs in these areas, true beliefs can be a source of unhappiness, at least for a time. This can be one way that rationality leads to unhappiness rather than happiness. But other beliefs also enter in, and a desire to seek truth, even painful truth, can itself take on a moral character, and provide a certain sense of meaning, even when one resolutely avoids supernatural falsehoods.

More broadly, a sense of meaning can come from nearly any project that one embraces and pursues. For although naturalism destroys the notions of meaning that could be built on religion, it seems that many of our feelings have little need for such abstractions, and can be adequately rooted in only the goals we choose and the actions we take. And those who are inclined can pick goals and actions with an eye toward our moral sensibilities. For while nothing in the wider universe constrains us to help each other or fight injustice or ease suffering, certainly nothing bars us from choosing such goals for ourselves.

This will never amount to the grand external meaning and morality of our religions and intuitions. But for those pursuing truth, it will have to do.

---

65. In geological or cosmological terms we arose only very, very recently. I am not suggesting that this fact proves any particular thesis. Rather the relevance of this fact is that there are many theses that we've rejected that involve seeing humanity as the center or purpose of things, and such theses are undermined by our recency.

66. Phrases about our minds being created or built or shaped are never meant to imply any sort of intention or teleology in that creating or building or shaping, but only to refer to how the mechanistic and unguided processes of evolution have slowly and aimlessly played out.

67. I intend this phrase as a reflection of the general workings of evolution, with selective pressures favoring only what aids survival and reproduction in a particular environment, and with it being in principle incidental if selection during a given evolutionary moment fits into larger selective trends, or if those larger trends result in something particularly complex or impressive or unusual, such as the human mind. I don't intend here to make any claims about which aspects of our minds do or do not directly help us to survive and reproduce, either presently or in our evolutionary past, and in that sense are or are not incidental.

68. To state things more fully, the matter concerns the entirety of our psychology, as molded by evolution, encoded in our genes, and taking shape in part through culture, social structures, upbringing, and individual choice; and how, across the differences between individuals and between groups, there are commonalities and resemblances in how we tend to react to various descriptions of reality.

69. When making life choices we never have perfect information, and so our choices always retain the character of a wager. Accepting this fact can lessen the agony and paralysis some people feel in the face of important decisions. It can also bring comfort after a particular life wager turns out to be a losing one.

70. These brief words point to what can be a massive and protracted personal undertaking.

71. Certainly such things can help some people toward these goals in some ways. And a great deal of unhappiness comes at least partly from failures to understand oneself, to understand others, and to understand the world, so that improving such understanding works against such unhappiness. But I am not making any general claims that rationality and clarity make people happier or more successful, and in fact I acknowledge ways they can do the opposite.

72. I mean that this is a central function for which language evolved, but not that it is the only function.

73. Or at the least they result from mental features that help us do such things, or that helped us to do them in the environments where we did most of our evolving.

74. By happiness I mean roughly one's overall subjective pleasure, contentment, or well-being, with physical pleasures and pains being part of the picture, but with other pleasures and pains also accounted for, including those relating to a person's values, attitudes, and beliefs.

# Author Biography

Phil Smoke was born in Michigan in 1986 and spent most of his time since then asking questions. He was intensely religious for a decade, devouring scripture and theology and philosophy, and learning practical lessons in service, organizing, and persuasion. His views changed and his studies continued, from biology to psychology to history and more, alongside degrees in philosophy, education, business, and law. His writings draw together all these disciplines and discourses to reach striking conclusions about the world and our place in it.

# ACADEMIC AND SPECIALIST

Iff Books publishes non-fiction. It aims to work with authors and titles that augment our understanding of the human condition, society and civilisation, and the world or universe in which we live.
If you have enjoyed this book, why not tell other readers by posting a review on your preferred book site.
Recent bestsellers from Iff Books are:

## Why Materialism Is Baloney

How true skeptics know there is no death and fathom answers to life, the universe, and everything
Bernardo Kastrup
A hard-nosed, logical, and skeptic non-materialist metaphysics, according to which the body is in mind, not mind in the body.
Paperback: 978-1-78279-362-5 ebook: 978-1-78279-361-8

## The Fall

Steve Taylor
*The Fall* discusses human achievement versus the issues of war, patriarchy and social inequality.
Paperback: 978-1-78535-804-3 ebook: 978-1-78535-805-0

## Brief Peeks Beyond

Critical essays on metaphysics, neuroscience, free will, skepticism and culture
Bernardo Kastrup
An incisive, original, compelling alternative to current mainstream cultural views and assumptions.
Paperback: 978-1-78535-018-4 ebook: 978-1-78535-019-1

# Framespotting

Changing how you look at things changes how
you see them

Laurence & Alison Matthews

A punchy, upbeat guide to framespotting. Spot deceptions and
hidden assumptions; swap growth for growing up. See and be free.

Paperback: 978-1-78279-689-3 ebook: 978-1-78279-822-4

# Is There an Afterlife?

David Fontana

Is there an Afterlife? If so what is it like? How do Western ideas
of the afterlife compare with Eastern? David Fontana presents the
historical and contemporary evidence for survival of
physical death.

Paperback: 978-1-90381-690-5

# Nothing Matters

a book about nothing

Ronald Green

Thinking about Nothing opens the world to everything by
illuminating new angles to old problems and stimulating new
ways of thinking.

Paperback: 978-1-84694-707-0 ebook: 978-1-78099-016-3

# Panpsychism

The Philosophy of the Sensuous Cosmos

Peter Ells

Are free will and mind chimeras? This book, anti-materialistic but
respecting science, answers: No! Mind is foundational
to all existence.

Paperback: 978-1-84694-505-2 ebook: 978-1-78099-018-7

**Punk Science**
Inside the Mind of God
Manjir Samanta-Laughton
Many have experienced unexplainable phenomena; God, psychic
abilities, extraordinary healing and angelic encounters. Can
cutting-edge science actually explain phenomena
previously thought of as 'paranormal'?
Paperback: 978-1-90504-793-2

**The Vagabond Spirit of Poetry**
Edward Clarke
Spend time with the wisest poets of the modern age and of the
past, and let Edward Clarke remind you of the importance of
poetry in our industrialized world.
Paperback: 978-1-78279-370-0 ebook: 978-1-78279-369-4


Readers of ebooks can buy or view any of these bestsellers by
clicking on the live link in the title. Most titles are published in
paperback and as an ebook. Paperbacks are available in traditional
bookshops. Both print and ebook formats are available online.
Find more titles and sign up to our readers' newsletter at
http://www.johnhuntpublishing.com/non-fiction
Follow us on Facebook at
https://www.facebook.com/JHPNonFiction
and Twitter at https://twitter.com/JHPNonFiction